D0893274

THE BAUSELL
HOME LEARNING GUIDE

Teach Your Child to Write

THE BAUSELL
HOME LEARNING GUIDE

Teach Your Child to Write

R. Barker Bausell, Ph.D.,
Carole R. Bausell, M.Ed.,
and Nellie B. Bausell, M.S.

Illustrations by Terry Dalton Kelly
Cartoons by Ruth Burke

THE SAUNDERS PRESS
W. B. Saunders Company
Philadelphia • London • Toronto

THE SAUNDERS PRESS
W.B. Saunders Company
West Washington Square
Philadelphia, PA 19105

IN THE UNITED STATES
DISTRIBUTED TO THE TRADE BY
HOLT, RINEHART AND WINSTON
383 Madison Avenue
New York, New York 10017

IN CANADA
DISTRIBUTED BY
HOLT, RINEHART AND WINSTON
55 Horner Avenue
Toronto, Ontario
M8Z 4X6
Canada

© 1980 by W. B. Saunders Company

Library of Congress Cataloging in Publication Data

Bausell, R. Barker,
The Bausell home learning guide.

1. English language — Composition and exercises —
Handbooks, manuals, etc.   2. Domestic education —
Handbooks, manuals, etc.   I. Bausell, Carole R.,   joint author.
II. Bausell, Nellie B.,   joint author.   III. Title.
LB1528.B28   649'.68   80-50716

ISBN 0-7216-1596-1 (Saunders)
ISBN 0-03-057666-0 (Holt, Rinehart & Winston)

Print Number 9 8 7 6 5 4 3 2 1

First Edition

TO THE MEMORY OF A DEDICATED TEACHER
Rufus B. Bausell

Acknowledgments

We would like to thank the following people for their help in the preparation of this book: Dr. Paul R. Daniels of The Johns Hopkins University for his teachings, ideas, and unsurpassed expertise in the area of language arts; Walt DelGiorno for his many excellent ideas; Dr. Thomas Horn for his kind permission to reprint portions of the spelling list from his father's classic work (*Progress in Spelling* by Drs. Ernest Horn and Ernest J. Ashbaugh); Carol Meyers for her aid in helping us prepare the manuscript; and the following Delaware public school teachers for their invaluable aid in helping us collect samples of children's writings—Kathy Lekites, Mary Powell, Helen Dixon, Doris Jenkins, Paulette Paterson, Joan Myer, Linda Conner, Dorothy Gibson, and Ethel Ellingsworth.

We would also like to acknowledge Terry Dalton Kelly for all the illustrations in this book with exception of the two cartoons in Chapter Four prepared by Ruth Burke.

Finally, we would like to sincerely acknowledge the support and guidance of our editor, Howard E. Sandum, without whose vision this work would not have been possible.

Contents

THE BAUSELL
HOME LEARNING GUIDE

Teach Your Child to Write

1

Teaching Your Child to Write

Writing, historically the second of the "Three R's," is a basic skill in name only. Despite continual complaints from business leaders, college professors, and parents, writing does not receive the attention it deserves in our schools' curriculum. For every dollar spent on reading, less than one *cent* is devoted to writing instruction.

This problem is documented most clearly by a recent Ford Foundation Report[1]. A survey of a large sample of seventeen-year olds showed that only one-fourth had received a written assignment more often than once every two weeks. The situation was even more extreme in elementary school where children averaged only one composition *per month*.

There is growing evidence, based both on surveys of teachers and of students, that our schools may be totally abandoning the teaching of composition. Leading educational journals are full of analyses of the problem such as Timothy Shanahan's recent report in *Phi Delta Kappan* in which a number of reasons for the crisis are suggested:

---

1. D. H. Graves. *Balance the Basics: Let Them Write.* 1979.

First, writing instruction in the elementary curriculum has been accorded a status so low that teachers are often uncertain whether they are supposed to teach writing. This reflects limitations both in teacher training and in instructional materials. . . . Second, writing is currently assigned a rather insignificant amount of instructional time. I think it is axiomatic that, unless the actual amount of writing instruction increases, writing will not improve.[2]

Is it really surprising, therefore, that verbal scores on the Scholastic Aptitude Test dropped 33 points from 1968 to 1978; that many recent Ph.D.s cannot spell, much less write, intelligently, and, perhaps worst of all, that this state of affairs is gradually becoming the accepted standard by which future performance will be judged?

What has happened to writing instruction? Certainly no one familiar with the academic and business worlds would argue that it is not important for a child's future success. The higher one rises in any career ladder, the more important writing ability becomes.

Fueled by the growing power of the testing establishment (mostly notably the Educational Testing Service of Princeton, New Jersey) as well as time constraints imposed on teachers by large classes, writing has become a casualty of the short-answer test. Today students tend to be evaluated primarily on the basis of multiple-choice examinations which require absolutely no writing on the part of the student and are therefore easy to correct by either teacher or computer.

As a result children are taught neither to write nor to *value* writing. Later, in more advanced courses of study, when the primary form of evaluation does become the term paper or essay examination, the effects are disastrous. The student who cannot write competently is severely handicapped, and there is very little he can do about it long after his *one* required freshmen composition or Remedial English Course and even longer after his monthly elementary school writing assignments.

In most forms of professional life, similar problems appear. People are aware of the publish-or-perish syndrome for college professors. Scholarly articles must be written in order to maintain

---

2. T. Shanahan. "The Writing Crisis: A Survey and a Solution." *Phi Delta Kappan,* 1979. *61,* 216-217.

one's job. But on a more practical level, consider the crucial role routine inter-office memoranda, written communications with clients, letters of application, and reports play in all other professional and managerial careers! For better or worse, the *way* the contents of these communiques are written often has as much impact as the actual substance involved, inviting quick but lasting judgments concerning the individuals who wrote them.

It may be here in professional life, in fact, that your child ultimately must pay the most costly price for failing to learn to write well. Everywhere we turned, everything we read, and everyone with whom we've discussed the subject has lamented the inability of recent college graduates to express themselves articulately and coherently in writing. This inability has, and will have, an impact not only upon individual careers but also upon the quality of all our lives. None of us is untouched by the productivity, efficiency, and competency of our industrial, business, academic, and health professionals. The very life of our country and our culture is affected. We allow the extinction of our writing tradition at our own peril, or as Thomas G. Wheeler in *The Great American Writing Block, Causes and Cures of the New Illiteracy* (Viking Press, 1979) succinctly states:

> Without clear thinking and coherent writing, no society can function properly. The widespread ability to write . . . is an underpinning that the technological age tries to destroy but needs for its survival.

Talking in terms of entire societies and cultures, however, tends to make the problem appear more remote than it really is. There is nothing distant nor hypothetical about the extremely crucial role writing will play in *your* child's personal future and in the development of his intellect. When a child unveils on paper his feelings and reactions toward an event, he learns and grows through the process itself. The very act often yields a finished product containing insights that simply did not exist prior to putting pen to paper. Writing is a thought process; learning to write is one way of learning to think.

Writing is also a means of self-expression and of self-fulfillment. A child can derive tremendous satisfaction from communicating in a medium that can be changed and honed until he is able to express what he feels, and that will remain long after those feelings would normally have been forgotten. It can also serve as a means of self-understanding, as a release of pent-up anxieties, fears, and emotions. Most of all, however, writing can be a source of unmitigated fun. Because that should be reason enough to teach it, we are led back to the original question: Why is writing so undervalued in the schools' curriculum?

We believe the answer lies in the nature of the discipline itself. Mechanical aspects of writing, such as spelling and penmanship, are easily taught to a large group of children at one time. Writing itself, however, is a difficult subject to teach, requiring much detailed, *individual* exchange. Since writing is an art as well as a skill, it is not easily reduced to parts which can be graded as either correct or incorrect; it is a language skill, and like all language skills, it requires continuous practice begun as early as possible.

In many ways, learning to write is similar to learning to play the piano. It is hard to imagine a child being able to play any piece of music well if only mechanical skills have been taught, such as finger placement or note recognition, especially in a class of thirty or more children. It is also hard to imagine a child truly excelling at the piano without both frequent lessons and practice starting in early childhood.

In this respect, writing is like playing the piano. It is not a skill most children pick up spontaneously and today this is even more true than in generations past. Daily opportunities and incentives to write have been far fewer since the telephone replaced the need for most letter writing in the home. The workbook assignment with accompanying multiple choice tests accomplished the same in the school.

The result, then, is that children increasingly are unable to express themselves in writing. Given the characteristics of the subject and the constraints under which the schools operate, we therefore believe the most logical place for serious writing instruction to occur, indeed the only place that it can really occur effectively, is in the home.

Our Philosophy of Teaching Writing

Until now we have talked about writing as though it were academically one subject. Really there are two quite separate parts to it. One involves self-expression. The other consists of skills which enable the writer to better express his thoughts and, thus, better communicate with his reader.

These two instructional paths begin separately but run parallel to one another with greater emphasis upon the first. Gradually, when they can no longer be separated, they will merge and the *skills* the child has learned along the way become the very *means* of self-expression.

The reason we advocate separating the teaching of writing mechanics from the self-expressive aspects relates to certain realities of human nature. A child can learn to print by practicing letter formations. Spelling can be learned by memorizing letter-sound correspondences in individual words. The child can only learn to express himself in writing, however, by actually putting something down on paper. The "something" is the child's thoughts, feelings, views, opinions, hopes, dreams—in a sense, a soul laid bare.

The written word leaves the writer extremely vulnerable. If the child says something orally with which others disagree, he can always argue, say he didn't mean it, that he was misunderstood, take it back, protest he didn't think about what he was saying, or simply deny saying it in the first place. In talking, there will always be another chance. Once something is in writing, however, defenses are harder to manufacture. So when the child's early attempts at writing are criticized, he may very well take it as a personal attack on his intelligence or his personality.

What we are saying is that we don't want you to be a "red pencil" teacher who ignores the message in favor of correcting the medium. The surest way to turn a child against writing is to pick on misspelled words, grammatical misusages, and printing abnormalities in a composition into which that child has poured his soul to describe something of great personal importance. These same skills can and should be taught, but not when the composition itself is used as the focal point.

Children should always be made to feel that their parents are interested in them. For that reason, the early efforts at self-expression should be a *no-lose proposition.* We believe in teaching the child to enjoy expressing himself, to *know* that efforts will be met with appreciation and interest even before the pencil is picked up. Only after the child is supremely self-confident in his writing ability should one begin to examine the compositions with an eye toward improving technical matters such as spelling, grammar, and

FIGURE 1-1

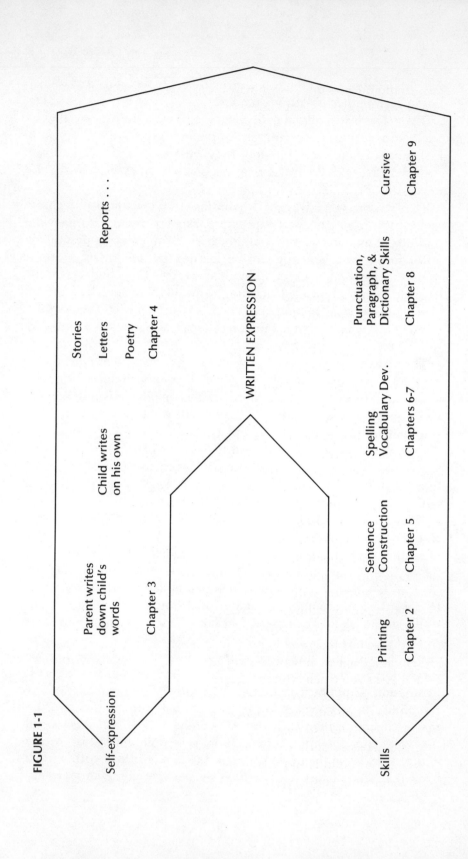

punctuation. Even that, as we will show you, can be done in a very non-threatening, subtle manner.

How to Use This Book

This book is separated into two tracks which are to be followed simultaneously. All parents are to read Chapters Three and Four. They make up the core of the book, containing numerous writing strategies and activities which encourage self-expression. (A few activities in Chapter Three may be too elementary for some children; others, however, address issues of importance for *all* children such as story dictation, playing with the typewriter, and constructing a picture dictionary.)

The remainder of the book is devoted to writing skills. You will devote certain days to these lessons, others to the actual creative writing activities in Chapters Three and Four. Chapter Two and Chapters Five through Nine progress from the most basic skills (some of which can be taught to preschool children) to more complex topics not normally mastered until the third grade. You will need to leaf through these chapters to decide which contain sections appropriate to your child's current level of development. Practically every chapter, however, does have at least one section which will be applicable to a wide developmental range, thus we encourage you to "shop around" since *you should not wait to complete any one chapter before teaching a relevant lesson contained in another.* (One exception to this is Chapter Nine, *Cursive Writing,* which should be reserved for the older child.)

Before you actually begin to teach your child, we want you to familiarize yourself with the rules of the game. In the first place there are none regarding the exact age at which any given child can profit from any given activity: individual differences between children are just too great to permit generalization. There *are* rules for you as a teacher, however. You must maintain your enthusiasm for the tasks you teach, you must make your child *feel* successful no matter how little he seems to learn on any given day, and you must avoid tiring him with overly long lessons. Whatever you do, *don't pressure your child to learn.*

If you are constantly confronted with inattentiveness it may be because your child is too young for, or simply unable to perform, the assignments you have set for him. If this happens we suggest that you either delay instruction or concentrate on more elementary tasks. To force teaching upon a child not yet ready to learn will only result in his disliking the subject and that is far worse than no teaching at all. Writing should be approached in the same spirit in which you read to, play, or take a trip with your child. Assume, in other words, that the two of you will enjoy the experience. If you are able to do this, teaching your child can be one of the most rewarding activities that will ever happen to either of you.

Getting Some Help

As a way of helping you with the important task you are about to undertake, the authors of this book would like to offer the following service. If at any time you have a question concerning your child's home writing instruction, send us your question in a self-addressed, stamped envelope and we will be happy to advise you. Address the question, and any material you may need to include, to:

Dr. R. Barker Bausell
P.O. Box 19109
Towson, MD 21204

2

Teaching your child to print.

The child who learns to print enters an exciting venture into the grown-up world. Children love to do anything they see older children and adults do, so little effort is usually needed to get them interested in writing. Because there are degrees of interest, we hope you will use your ideas and ingenuity to develop enthusiasm for the task.

The Importance of Play

Children learn and practice much of what they need to know in life when they play. This includes the perceptual-motor skills which will be used in learning to print. Writing of course, involves fine motor skills to a great extent and presupposes a certain developmental level before it makes much sense to institute a great deal of formal instruction. Very young children, as we all know, are quite awkward with small objects like pencils or crayons and much more comfortable with large ones like blocks or balls. As they grow older, however, their natural curiosity leads them to manipulate more and more types of objects. This continual interaction with the environment increasingly results in the ability to handle smaller and smaller objects in a more functional fashion.

Although vast individual differences exist, below is an example of the order in which some of the more common perceptual-motor skills might develop in a typical child. Please be aware that these are only estimates based on developmental scales[1] and as such should not be interpreted literally.

DEVELOPMENTAL MILESTONES

Time in Months	Gross Motor	Fine Motor
10		Explores parts of toys, probing holes and grooves
12 (1 yr.)	Throws or rolls a ball	
14		
16		Pats pictures in book, helps turn pages, stacks 2 blocks
18		Scribbles with pencil if placed in hand, initiates strokes with crayon
20	Begins to run and jump (can't clear floor when jumping)	Builds tower with 5-6 blocks
22		Imitates vertical line within 30 degrees
24 (2 yrs.)	Can kick a ball	Snips with scissors, turns single page in book, imitates circular strokes with crayon
26		
28		
30		Copies circle (2½-3 yrs.)
32		
34		
36 (3 yrs.)	Catches large ball with arms out straight; rides tricycle	Unbuttons accessible buttons Draws and names simple figures Draws a figure with head and legs

---

1. Items have been adapted from numerous developmental scales including those of Verna Hart, Arnold Gesell, Mildred Berry, Rebecca Flaharty, and the Denver Developmental Test.

Time in Months	Gross Motor	Fine Motor
38		
40		
42	Runs smoothly	Picks longer line
44		
46		
48 (4 yrs.)	Throws ball overhand	Draws straight line, copies cross
60 (5 yrs.)	Skips, uses roller skates and sled	Draws figure with 3-6 parts (4-5 yrs.)
72 (6 yrs.)	Knows right and left (6-7 yrs.)	Can print a few letters, copies rectangles (5)

It may still surprise many people how early the average child is able to put pencil to paper. You can *greatly* facilitate the progression of fine motor skills by patiently encouraging your child's early desire to touch, feel, and manipulate everything he sees and *by providing appropriate opportunities for practicing fine motor skills*.

You should continue to provide the opportunities and tools needed to engage in stimulating, productive play. In the fine motor area these might include: crayons, paste, paper, coloring books, tracing paper, scissors, puzzles, and so forth. Encourage a balance between them and more active, but equally important, games involving throwing a ball, jumping, running, and climbing.

Let the child know that you value, are proud of, and are interested in all his accomplishments. On one day he might have a drawing to show you, on another a new way he learned to jump rope. These lessons are as important as the ones you are about to teach and the social interaction they afford will help make your child get along better in the classroom.

How to Use This Chapter

This chapter consists of twenty-six lessons designed to teach your child to print the twenty-six letters of the alphabet in both upper (capitalized) and lower case formats. Some previous experiences with letters, such as seeing them in print or being able to recite the ABC jingle, will make this process easier. It is by no means necessary, however, that the child actually know his letters before proceeding with this chapter. (Should you wish to teach letter recognition first, we suggest that you refer to Chapter Four of *Teach Your Child to Read.*)

Read the general suggestions for teaching your child and the description of the activities in the basic lesson format. Next, study the Model Lesson. It is the only lesson with detailed instructions on how to apply the basic lesson format. The remaining lessons may be taught exactly the same way, or you may improvise on them as you become more at ease with teaching and more attuned to your child's needs.

Each lesson contains three basic parts. Part I deals with the introduction of the capital letter to be learned, tracing and writing exercises involving it and memorization of its formation. Part II exactly repeats these steps for the lower case form of the letter. Part III involves practice, review of both capital and lower case forms and meaningful word activities that are highly enjoyable. In addition, there are optional supplementary activities for the child who needs extra practice or a slower pace.

Determining when to teach these lessons. It is crucial that you not require or expect more of your child than he is capable of producing. Individual differences are so great between children that it is simply impossible to tell you when to teach the lessons and activities contained in this chapter without personal knowledge of *your* child.

Fortunately, no one knows your child better than you, thus no one is in a better position to decide when to teach what, nor how much to expect, as long as you adopt our one overriding rule: *caution.* Be conservative. If you are introducing the letters to a very young child for the first time, be happy with *any* resemblance of his creations to the real thing. You may, in fact, decide only to teach a few letters, such as the ones in his name, and only then to use the section in Part I titled "Introducing the Letter" which teaches recognition of the capital form and provides a very informal introduction to writing. If you are working with an older child, such as a kindergartener, you may wish to teach the "Introducing the Letter" section in both Parts I and II as well as the "Adding Meaning" exercises, saving the rest for later. Suffice it to say that there are no rules other than to be cautious, patient, and to remember that your child does not need to know how to print before proceeding to the actual writing activities in Chapters Three and Four.

Determining which lessons to teach. This chapter contains lessons for all the letters of the alphabet. If you suspect that your child can form some of the letters, find out which ones are known before beginning. To do this, simply give him a pencil and a piece of lined paper (see "Materials" section below) and say something like:

Can you print a big "A"? (Make sure that no letter models, such as an alphabet strip, are in his line of sight to copy.)

When this is accomplished:

How about a little "a"?

Continue this process for the remainder of the alphabet (occasionally skipping around) or until you are reasonably sure which letters the child cannot form. Evaluating the results must be a subjective process since he may know some letters but make them poorly. The best advice we can give you at this point is to compare each of your child's letters to the following chart and ask yourself whether (1) all the necessary strokes are there and the proper size observed, and (2) your child's teacher (or future teacher) is likely to be satisfied. Remember that no one prints letters perfectly, and young children's writing does look shaky. If you are in doubt, we suggest that you go ahead and teach the printing of a particular letter.

Once you have evaluated the results of this test you should write out the alphabet in upper and lower case formats (that is, Aa Bb . . . Zz) and circle those letters that the child does not know. Keep this record, along with your child's actual performance, in a safe place in order to check progress from time to time. In fact, the test may be repeated at any time. Both you and the child will enjoy

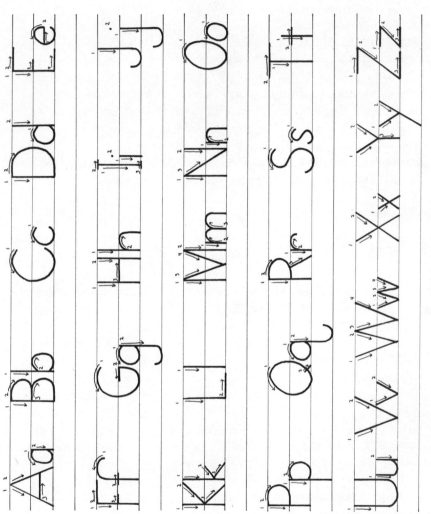

ALPHABET CHART

comparing the handwriting after instruction to the attempts before you began.

Depending upon his present knowledge, you should pursue one of the following courses of action:

1. If no letters are known, begin with the model lesson and proceed through the lessons in order.
2. If some letters are known and others are not, mark those lessons dealing with the unknown letters and teach them in the order in which they are presented in this chapter.
3. If one form of a letter is known and the other is not (for example, if your child can print a capital "A" but cannot print the lower case version), then you need only teach the part of the lesson pertaining to the unknown format *plus* the activities listed in Part III of that lesson.
4. If all the letters are adequately formed, proceed to Chapters Three and Four or any of the remaining supplementary chapters upon which your child needs work.

There is no reason why you need to finish all twenty-six lessons before proceeding to the actual writing activities presented in Chapters Three and Four. Both chapters provide opportunities for the child to *dictate* his thoughts for you to print. Children are capable of written expression long before they master all the necessary handwriting and spelling skills, so by all means intersperse some of the activities presented in those chapters with the lessons in this one.

General Suggestions

Here are some guiding principles which will make teaching easier for you and more effective for your child:

1. **Be prepared.** Each lesson in this chapter requires the preparation of exercise sheets in advance. Make sure that you prepare these sheets, set out all the other materials you will need, and read over the lesson outline *before* you actually sit down for the teaching session. Not having to do these things during the lesson will make it a lot easier to teach and will help to increase your child's attention span as well.

2. **Don't work beyond your child's attention span.** Your

child's attention span will vary according to his age, personality, mood, the amount of sleep he got the night before, how active his day has been, how long ago his last meal was, and any number of other factors. Your attention span and motivation will vary along similar lines as well, although fortunately not as drastically.

There is no way that we can tell you exactly how many minutes each particular lesson should take. There is no reason why you should have to complete a lesson every time you sit down with your child, nor is there any reason why you should end a session just because a lesson has been completed. Each lesson is divided into independent activities in order to provide natural stopping places. We do recommend, however, that you sit down together frequently, if for only brief periods. You are in no hurry and you will be surprised at how much progress can be made working fifteen minutes per day five days per week.

Since you know your child, you will recognize the signs that signal the approach of boredom. Quit before the lesson becomes tedious. You have a lot to teach. Quitting a few minutes early now and then isn't going to make much difference in the long run as to how much is learned. It can make a great deal of difference, however, in how much the two of you enjoy the process.

3. **Be flexible.** Although the lesson format has been designed to fit the needs of as many children as possible, all children are different and you are in the best position to know your child. Once you have mastered the basic procedures suggested in the model lesson, use this knowledge to tailor these materials to your child's needs. Teaching your own child at home is the ultimate in individualized instruction. Capitalize on it every chance you get.

If it is obvious to you that your child has learned to print a letter before you have finished all the prescribed activities, then go on to the next part of the lesson. If the script for an activity doesn't reflect the way you and your child talk, then by all means rephrase it. If we use a word that you don't think is in your child's vocabulary, then substitute one that is. In other words, improvise. Be creative.

4. **Be goal-oriented.** Although flexibility as a means to an end is fine, never lose sight of what you are trying to teach in each particular lesson. It is very easy to get side-tracked and forget both your immediate and ultimate purposes. Some children, in fact, are quite adept at inducing forgetfulness in their parents and teachers. Don't let it happen.

5. **Keep your instruction low key.** You can't pressure a child to learn. If you do we'll guarantee that he won't.

It's just as easy to make learning fun as it is to make it terrible. Be positive and avoid sarcasm at all costs. It is, of course, necessary to tell a child when he makes a mistake. Children don't mind this if it is done kindly and constructively. Point out things that are correct as well as those that need improvement. Always structure the lesson so that your child is sure to succeed at *something* regardless of how slowly he seems to be learning the things you are teaching. (The structured writing activities in this chapter should be especially helpful in this regard.)

You must always keep in mind that you may be teaching a great deal more than the contents of the individual lessons contained in this book. You may very well be teaching how either to enjoy or to detest learning *itself*. The accomplishment of the first is far more important than anything else you can teach; the accomplishment of the second is far worse than not teaching a child at all.

6. **Don't expect perfection.** As we have stated before, writing is partly a learned and partly a developmental process. A young child is not going to print a letter as accurately as an adult no matter how much instruction he receives. This is one of the reasons that you should *not* attempt to finish this chapter before beginning the next one, another is that only so many practice exercises can be given before boredom sets in. Generally speaking, as you progress through the other chapters in this book, the child will receive enough practice to eventually print all his letters with reasonable accuracy.

7. **Don't teach writing in a vacuum.** In many ways writing and reading are not separate subjects at all, but only phases on a continuum. It really makes very little sense to teach either one in isolation, as we will stress throughout this book. Ideally, you will teach the two together. At the very least, you should point out the relationships between the two every chance you get.

8. **Follow a regular schedule.** Although there is nothing more natural than teaching your own child, there are some things that are easier. If you are not careful, you may eventually find a way to take the easier course.

What we recommend, therefore, is that you choose a regular time and place for your teaching sessions and adhere to that schedule each day. Choose a place in your home as free from distractions as possible. Take the phone off the hook if necessary, turn off the television, and do whatever else is necessary to assure concentration on the part of your child. Once the two of you have settled into this sort of routine, your sessions together will become something the child can look forward to and count on.

Basic Lesson Format

Because a great deal more is involved, we have designed a lesson format that encourages not only finger movements but also the essential memorization, patience, and concentrative processes as well. In addition, instead of teaching the letters entirely by rote, the child learns to combine letters into familiar words as early as the seventh lesson. In this way he learns from the start that there is an important purpose to these strange little chicken scratches; he begins to see that writing is another way to communicate meaning.

The steps of the lesson format are outlined below and then explained. They will become more clear when you see them applied in the Model Lesson that follows. All the lessons in this chapter are taught using basically the same format, so once you have taught a couple of letters, the routine will become automatic. The outline will serve as a continual reminder of the steps to follow.

Introducing the letter. (Applies to capital and lower case, Parts I and II). The letters are not presented alphabetically (that is from A to Z), but rather in a sequence in which those easier to learn and more commonly used are introduced first. Easier letters are generally those made from straight lines and those in which the capital and lower case formats are similar. **L-1**, for example, is easier than **R-r** because only straight lines are involved; **O-o** is easier than **D-d** because upper and lower case O's are the same shape; **X-x** and **Z-z** are also relatively easy because they involve both similar formats and straight lines. (X and Z occur less frequently in children's reading, however, so are taught later.)

Since the letters are not presented in alphabetical order, it is important to locate each letter within the context of the alphabet. Toward this end, you will need to make (or purchase) an *alphabet strip*, which is nothing more than a long narrow piece of white poster board on which the alphabet is printed in order. (See Materials).

Aa Bb Cc .... Zz

Once the letter being taught has been introduced and situated within the alphabet via the alphabet strip, its shape is discussed and informally traced with the index finger. The child is then shown how to write the letter with crayon in large, bold strokes on an *unlined* writing surface. (The capital formation is taught in Part I, followed by its lower case counterpart in Part II.)

Tracing and writing. (Applies to capital and lower case, Parts I and II.) Each lesson includes exercises for you to construct on sheets of tablet paper. They indicate the *correct sequence of strokes* or the exact way in which the letter is to be made, and take the child from partial tracing to independent writing.

This particular step in the writing process requires a great deal of attention on the part of the parent to insure that the correct sequence of strokes is *always* followed. This means that although a small "a" has both a circular stroke and a straight line, the straight line is never made before the circular stroke. The prescribed order is always observed. On the other hand, you may have your own way of forming a certain letter; obviously, there are many acceptable ways to reach the same outcome. The method that we recommend, however, has been used by teachers everywhere for many years and found to be sound for children. It is *crucial* that the child *consistently* use the same sequence of strokes in learning to write, whether you teach our formations or your own. It is equally important to show your patience during this process and your enthusiasm for small signs of progress. He will need both these qualities in you to develop his own concentration needed for successful completion of this chapter.

Memorization. (Applies to capital and lower case, Parts I and II.) After the child is able both to trace and to copy a letter on an exercise sheet, it is time for him to learn to make the letter unaided by a model. There is only one way to do that and it is through memorization.

The particular method we suggest involves (1) looking at the model, (2) copying it, (3) covering it up, (4) writing it again, (5) uncovering the model and checking the results. The entire process is repeated until a letter can be written accurately from memory. (This letter must be accurate not only in how the finished product looks but also in the degree to which the correct sequence of strokes was followed.)

Practice. (Part III.) You will provide practice as needed throughout the lesson. Here, however, we are referring to a formal activity in which both capital and lower case formats are written side-by-side several times on a tablet page. The objective is to help strengthen the association between the two formats so that they are recognized as representing the same letter.

Review. (Part III.) The need for review is a constant in all teaching, but it is especially important in initial writing. It is very easy for a child to quickly forget the fine points of these alien notations. Therefore in this section various games and exercises are suggested for reinforcing the concepts learned so far in the chapter.

Adding Meaning. (Part III.) This activity does not appear in the basic lesson format until Lesson No. 7, but from that point on becomes an essential part of the teaching-to-write process. Here the child joins letters to make familiar words. For the first time he begins learning to *write* in the full sense of the word. Also learned are the important subsidiary skills of spacing between words, using capitalization, and the most elemental literary form: the title.

The specific words that will be written are based not only on the letters introduced to that point, but also on their familiarity to children through speaking and early reading experience. (As we stated earlier, it is recommended that writing instruction be combined with reading instruction through a medium such as *Teach Your Child to Read.*)

Many words that could be formed fairly early are therefore intentionally omitted. Instead the child will be presented with a word that he can either already read or learn to read easily. It will then be used as a title for a picture which he will draw.

Structured Writing (optional). Some children have more difficulty learning to print than others. Structured Writing is designed only for the child who needs extra guidance with the mechanics of making the letters correctly. If general difficulty is encountered in the tracing and writing phase of each lesson, the structured writing activities can serve as a permanent substitute for Tracing and Writing (Activity #2) in all lessons. If *specific* difficulty is encountered only with particular letters, then the activities can serve as supplementary practice where needed.

There are children who *continue* to have special problems related to handwriting. These problems range from mild to severe and sometimes create serious academic difficulties for children no matter how bright they are. If administered soon enough (and in some cases that is no later than mid-second grade), the highly prescribed, structured activities presented in this part of the lesson are appropriate for such children as well. For severely disabled children, and those whose poor habits have gone uncorrected for years, the typewriter is probably the most helpful writing aid that can be used. (A more detailed description of special problems related to learning to print may be found at the end of this chapter; the use of the typewriter as well as a process we call "typesetting" are discussed in Chapter Three.)

The structured writing activities themselves are similar to the tracing exercises discussed earlier except there are many more of them and their progression from simple to complex is much more gradual. As important as it is everywhere in this chapter to follow instructions precisely, it is even more crucial here that you teach the child to follow the correct sequence of strokes for each and every exercise. When the child is confronted by a situation like this, for example, it is absolutely essential that he *"trace what's there"* first and then finish the remainder of the letter himself. The result is that the letter is made exactly the way you eventually want him to make it from start to finish with the correct sequence of strokes.

The second component of the structured writing activities that should be followed exactly is vocalization. For each exercise you should invent words describing the correct sequence of strokes and then repeat them with the child in unison until the strokes have been memorized. (For example, corresponding to capital "T" you would probably use the words "down, across" which describe the two pencil movements required in its construction.)

Writing Posture.

The child's writing posture has a good deal to do with how well the letters will be formed. You must pay especially careful attention to insuring proper hand and paper placement from the very beginning. Bad habits, once formed, are almost impossible to break.

The child should be comfortably seated at a desk or table with adequate lighting positioned so a shadow is not cast upon the writing page. The tablet page should be in front of the child, perpendicular to the body. Both arms need to rest on the desk top with the writing hand lying beneath the line of print to insure that the child can see what he is writing.

Right-handed. The paper should lie straight in front of the child or slightly to the right of the middle of his body. In either case it should be straight, not slanted. The right side of the heel of the writing hand, along with the nails of the last two fingers, rests on the desk as does the right forearm. The wrist on the other hand, lies close to the desk but does not touch it. As the child writes, his hand and arm glides to the right over the paper. The pencil is held in a loose grip just above the edge of the paint (about one inch from the point). The index finger rests on top while the pencil is supported between the thumb and inner side of the middle finger. The left hand holds the top left corner of the paper so that it doesn't tear or move out of position. As the writing progresses down the page, the left hand is used to move the paper up.

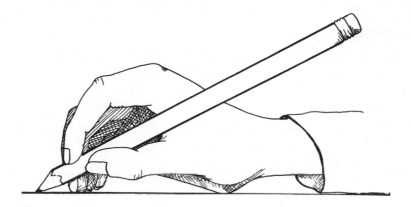

Left-handed. The paper lies slightly to the left of the middle of the body. As with the right-handed child the paper is straight, not slanted. The writing hand (left) holds the pencil a little further back, (one and a half inches from the point) than does that of the right-handed child so that during writing the hand does not block the child's view of the print. The hand is aligned with the forearm (wrist straight) just as with the right-handed child. *The hand should not be hooked around with a bent wrist.*

The right hand holds the upper right hand corner of the paper in place moving the page up as it is filled.

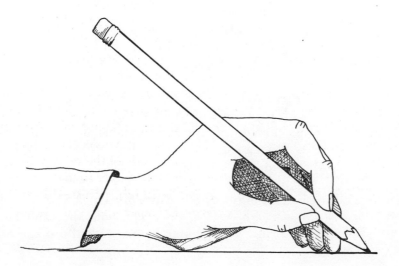

Materials

You will need the following aids for eacl lesson. You should always prepare whatever materials you will need prior to sitting down with your child.

1. **Unlined paper** for initial writing attempts. This can even be scrap paper or brown shopping bags slit open to lie flat. A chalkboard that can lie flat is also a possibility.
2. **Crayons.** Whatever size your child is used to is fine.
3. **Paper Tablet.** These should contain lines spaced approximately one inch apart and separated by a broken or very faint line. They are often called "practice tablets for beginners" and contain the alphabet set in primary type on their covers. They are usually available in drug and variety stores for considerably less than a dollar.
4. **Several sharpened pencils.** If you are working with a beginner, we recommend the use of primary pencils which are much larger in diameter than regular pencils and easier to hold. (Although some experts prefer starting the child with regular-sized pencils.) If your child is in school, use whatever type writing instruments are used there.
5. **Alphabet strip.** This is a long strip of paper (no longer than your desk top), upon which the alphabet is printed in order (see illustration page 19). We suggest white posterboard, both because of its durability and the resulting visibility of letters printed upon it. (Make sure you print the letters in the same style as taught in the lessons and shown in the illustration on page 14). A bright colored "magic marker" often adds visual appeal.

   Another good alternative to poster board is a yardstick covered with paper or *wide* masking tape adhered in a long strip across the top of the desk or table upon which you work. It is also a good idea to put up an alphabet wall chart somewhere the child spends a good deal of time, such as in the bedroom or family room.
6. **Letter cards.** A letter card consists of a blank 3" × 5" index card (or one cut in half) upon which both the capital and lower case forms of the letter being studied are carefully printed.

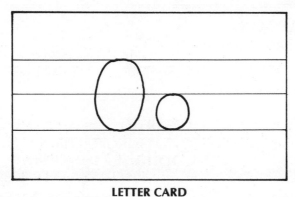

LETTER CARD

7. **Child's scissors.** Blunt ended.
8. **Children's paste.** The kind that is safe if ingested.
9. **Word cards.** A 3″ × 5″ index card on which the word the child learns is printed in advance (one word per card starting in Lesson 7).
10. **Exercises sheets.** Two tablet pages *prepared in advance* identically to illustrations on pages 28 and 33. To construct these sheets see page 38.
11. **Construction paper,** or other unlined paper for the illustrations called for in the "Adding Meaning" activities.
12. **Loose-leaf binder** or home-made cover in which illustrations may be inserted.

MODEL LESSON
Writing the Letter **Oo**

PART I

Capital O

ACTIVITY #1.
Introducing the letter **O**

Sit next to your child, preferably at a table or desk away from all distractions. If your child is right-handed, sit on his right. If he is left-handed, sit on his left.

Take out the alphabet strip (unless it is already taped to the desk top) and the letter card for **Oo.** Say something like:

Today we're going to learn to write one of the letters of the alphabet. Here is the one we're going to learn: **O.**

Show the letter card and point to the capital **O.**

Here is the big **O** *and here is little* **o.** *Do these letters look like a shape you know?* (Answer: a circle or a ball)

That's right. They're just like big and little circles (balls).

Take out the alphabet strip and say:

I'm going to say and point to each letter of the alphabet. Would you like to say them with me? (Even if the child doesn't know all the letter names yet, he may enjoy chiming in with the sound of his voice slightly trailing yours.)

Show the child the letter card and say:

I want you to stop me after I say the letter **Oo**. *Then I want you to put the letter card on top of it.* (This is an easy exercise which most children won't have any trouble with at all, so make a game out of it. If the **O** is recognized easily, compliment him. If not, show him by comparison with the letter card that you have indeed pointed to it.)

Next, take out the unlined paper and crayons and show how to make the letter. Let the child practice using various colors and bold strokes.

ACTIVITY #2.
Tracing and Writing

Take out the lined paper tablet upon which you have copied the Tracing and Writing exercise. Make sure that you make an exact copy of this exercise before the lesson. Place the page in front of the child (see above). Move your chair back and toward the child. Reach over his shoulder and trace the capital **O** slowly with the blunt end of a pencil several times calling attention to the point at which you start and to the direction in which you swing the line. (The direction is counter-clockwise but is best explained by telling the child to "swing over to the left" even if he doesn't yet know left from right.)

The first model **O** has a number 1 to show where to start and an arrow to illustrate the direction in which the pencil is moved. Explain what these marks mean so that the child will begin to become accustomed to the system we're using to illustrate how the model letters are formed.

Explain and demonstrate (by pointing and tracing with the blunt end of your pencil) on the model page that:

1. The capital **O** has only one line.
2. It is begun at the point where the number 1 lies and formed by one continuous circular stroke to the left.
3. Its size is dictated by the width of the top and bottom lines of the tablet page (that is, it is drawn within two bold faced

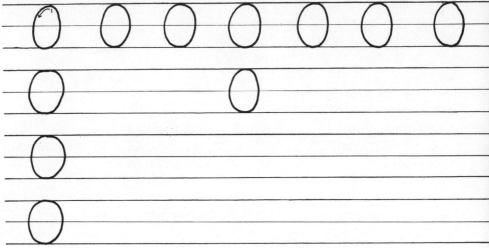

TRACING AND WRITING EXERCISE SHEET

lines, crossing over the broken or very faint middle line that lies between them).

If the child can already draw a circle, he will probably need very little help with this aspect of forming the letter.

*Are you ready to trace these big **O**'s with your pencil?*

Undoubtedly, he will be quite anxious to begin, so, using the writing end of the pencil, have the child trace over the model letters on the exercise sheet.

All the **O**'s in the top row should be traced in pencil slowly and correctly. Always remind the child to make the line in the correct direction. In the following rows the complete **O**'s which are drawn in should be traced in their entirety (you will note that there is always an **O** at the start of a row and sometimes one in the middle as well), and the others should be written by the child independently so that all the rows are filled. He should always progress across the page from left to right so that in the second row

(1) the first **O** is traced,
(2) two **O**'s are written unaided,
(3) the second model is traced, and
(4) two more **O**'s are written in the space remaining.

Provide additional practice pages as needed. Always place

several model **O**'s on the page and *watch carefully* to insure that they are all made properly. Your child may need a great deal of practice in just tracing the letters at this point. If you judge this to be the case, all you need do is to make additional rows modeled on our first one above, and allow him to trace as much as necessity and interest warrant. Be sure to praise his efforts.

If you should notice that he makes a few **O**'s well, but starts to have difficulty toward the end of a row, be sure to place a model **O** not only at the beginning of a line but also at the middle. At this stage of learning you can't allow the child to practice letter formation without supervision because you will need to see that he follows the correct sequence of strokes. Watch to be sure that the proper writing posture and position of paper and pencil are maintained.

ACTIVITY #3
Memorization

On a separate sheet of tablet paper write a model **O** on the first row at the left hand side. Have the child fill the row independently with **O**'s, then cover the row with a card or folded paper and instruct him to make the letter from memory on the second row. After each letter, have him check his work by removing the card and examining his original letters. Repeat this process until accurate **O**'s are reproduced from memory. Continue to observe that the stroke is made in the correct direction.

SUPPLEMENTARY ACTIVITY
Structured Writing

(To be employed only if the child continues to have great difficulty in forming the **O** on his own.)

Examine the illustration below, then compare is to the **O** column on page 46. You will note that we have included only

STRUCTURED WRITING EXERCISE SHEET

the five different approximations used for each letter. When you make structured writing exercise sheets for other letters, you will draw complete letters in both the entire first row and first column as shown above. (Place the numbers and arrows on the first letter by using the alphabet chart as your model, and add dots to show where the pencil first touches on all the letters in the first row and on the first letter in the second row). The remainder of the table will correspond to the **O** column on page 46. The second row on your exercise sheet will thus be made up of complete letters, the third row will contain the next most complete approximation, the fourth row the next most complete, and so on. An extra row should be added at the end where the child will draw the letter entirely on his own.

Once the exercise sheet has been constructed, you should illustrate to the child how the letters in the first row are to be traced using the blunt end of a pencil. Tell the child:

Always put your pencil on the dot and go where the numbers and arrows show. See, number 1 means I start here and follow this arrow.

(It may be that your child does not yet know his numbers or will have a good deal of difficulty following the arrows at first. Have patience and he will eventually get better at the process. In any case you will always be available to guide him.)

Let the child trace over the first three letters with the writing end of his pencil. As he traces each one, repeat the words you have invented to describe the correct sequence of strokes. In this case it might be: *Curve around—***O**

Tell him:

I say "curve around" because that's what you do with your pencil. I say **O** *because that's the name of the letter. Why don't you say it with me while you trace the rest of the* **O**'s *in this row?*

Watch each letter being traced to be sure the direction shown by the arrow is being observed. If it isn't, say:

Look, it goes this way. Demonstrate again with the blunt pencil end.

The child should be able to trace the last few letters in the first row by himself correctly *before* proceeding to the second row. If he doesn't, make additional rows, identical to the first, and have him practice until he can.

The first letter in the second row is made just like those in the previous row. The remaining letters, however, are only partially complete. For each of these the child should start the letter as usual and *trace what is there* before filling in the missing sections. In other words, he still makes the entire letter from start to finish. The only difference is that he is now responsible for finishing it without the help of tracing guidelines. (You will note that there is very little for him to complete on his own, however, and he should still be repeating the guide words "Curve Around **O**.") As with the first row, do not proceed to the next row unless this task has been completed without problems. If needed, provide additional practice on a separate piece of paper.

Each successive row is designed in such a way that more and more of the tracing lines are missing until in the final row they are absent altogether. In each case the child traces what is present before filling in the rest and in each case he observes the correct sequence of strokes from start to finish. The guide words are spoken throughout the entire exercise and are dropped only when the letter has been securely learned.

PART II

Little o

ACTIVITY #1
Introducing the O

Now that you know how to make big O, *little o will be very easy to learn.*

Show the letter card.

See how little o looks like big O *only smaller?*
Let's practice writing little o with crayons.

ACTIVITY #2
Tracing and Writing

Using the letter card, point out how little o only goes as high as the middle line. Next position your already prepared exercise sheet in front of the child, reach over his shoulder and trace the little o slowly with the blunt end of a pencil. Call attention again to the fact that it is formed in the same way as the capital O except it only reaches the middle line.

Explain and demonstrate on the exercise sheet that:

1. The little o has only one line.
2. It is begun at the point where the number 1 is drawn and formed by one continuous circular stroke to the left.

O O O O O O O

O O

O

O

TRACING AND WRITING EXERCISE SHEET

3. Its size is dictated by the distance between the middle and bottom lines of the tablet page (that is, its top touches the middle line, its base the bottom line).

Are you ready to trace over these little o's with your pencil?

Allow the child to trace over the model letters with the writing end of a pencil. Work through the model page and any additional practice pages necessary just as you did in Part I. If the child forgets where to start the letter, call his attention back to the number 1 in the first model or add numbers to his practice pages as guides. Always remember to show enthusiasm for these first efforts in written communication. Let him feel that he has made a big step forward in his life. He has.

ACTIVITY #3
Memorization

This activity is conducted identically to Activity #3 for the capital **O**. It consists of having the child:

1. write one row of small **o**'s using a model you have supplied,
2. covering that row and writing letters from memory,
3. checking his work by uncovering the first row, and
4. repeating the process until accurate small **o**'s are reproduced from memory.

SUPPLEMENTARY ACTIVITY
Structured Writing

(To be employed only if the child continues to have great difficulty in forming the small **o** from memory.)

As in Part I, this activity consists of the following steps:

1. The exercise sheet should be constructed on a blank tablet page based on the **o** column on page 48. Remember that the first two rows and the first column are composed of complete letters with the first letter in the chart having the number and arrow found in the alphabet chart.
2. Trace the letter with the blunt end of a pencil and show the child how the letters in the first row are to be traced.
3. Explain that the dot and number show where to start and the arrow illustrates direction.
4. Allow the child to trace over the first three letters with the writing end of his pencil. As this is done, say "curve-around—**o**" (or whatever you decide is the best way to verbalize the process.)
5. Have the child repeat "curve-around—**o**" as the rest of the letters in the first row are traced.
6. In each successive row have the first letter (which is always complete) traced in the same way and the partially completed letters traced over before completing the missing sections. Make sure the recommended sequence of strokes is followed for each exercise.
7. Administer extra practice whenever needed by constructing additional exercises for the child. Make sure that the guide words ("Curve Around—**o**") are repeated each time he forms the letter until it has been securely learned.

O O O O O

O O O O O

O C C C C

O ⌒ ⌒ ⌒ ⌒

O ⌝ ⌝ ⌝ ⌝

STRUCTURED WRITING EXERCISE SHEET

PART III

Practice and Review

ACTIVITY #1
Practice

The purpose of this activity is to bind the upper and lower case forms of the letters together in the child's mind since they have been studied in isolation to this point. All that is really involved is for you to prepare the first row of a tablet page so that there are four pairs of capital and lower case O's running across (that is, **Oo Oo Oo Oo**).

Next, discuss the similarities and differences in the two forms. With **O** this is very obvious since they differ only with respect to size. Have the letters in the first row traced and then copied independently on the remaining rows of the page.

ACTIVITY #2
Review

Review will not be necessary after the first couple of lessons given the small number of letters the child is dealing with. Thereafter, it will be included periodically as indicated.

ACTIVITY #3
Adding Meaning

This activity does not begin until Lesson 7.

TEACHING THE REMAINING LESSONS

The remaining letters should be taught following the same Basic Lesson Format presented in the model lesson. In this section we will give you some hints for applying that format to the rest of the letters in the alphabet. We will also discuss the "review" and "adding meaning" procedures, and present the order in which the letters will be taught.

Lesson Order

The order in which the letters are to be taught has been carefully planned to insure that as many commonly occurring, easy to form letters are taught first as possible. In order to reap the maximum benefit possible from this chapter it is important that you teach the letters in the following order:

LESSON 1.	Oo	LESSON 6.	Ee
LESSON 2.	Tt	LESSON 7.	Mm
LESSON 3.	Ll	LESSON 8.	Hh
LESSON 4.	Ii	LESSON 9.	Nn
LESSON 5.	Ff	LESSON 10.	Aa

Introducing the Letter: Other Examples

As in the model lesson, you will first show the letter form to the child on the letter card. After this initial step, however, there is a great deal of leeway for creativity.

The capital **T**, for example, can be illustrated with your hands by placing one vertically and the other horizontally; the lower case **t** can be illustrated via two crossed fingers; the capital **L** formed by two pencils; the lower case **l** by one finger or by the number one; and so forth.

Once each letter has been located within the alphabet strip you may discuss its formation more formally. The best way to do this is to refer to the alphabet chart and point out the way in which the letter is printed, the correct starting point for the pencil and the correct sequence of strokes.

In introducing the capital **T**, for example, you could refer to the exercise sheet you have made and point out that:

1. *The big **T** has two lines or sticks.*
2. *The tall stick is drawn first starting at the top line and pulling down,* (The arrow indicates the direction of a line; the number the order in which the lines are drawn.)
3. *The stick that lies on top is drawn across from left to right on the top line.* (Note the 2 and accompanying arrow.)

In introducing a more complex letter, such as the lower case **a**, the same procedure is followed. Simply refer the child to the exercise sheet you have prepared for that lesson while talking about the letter:

1. *Little* a *is made from a small circle and a short stick.*
2. *The small circle is made just like the letter* o. (You may illustrate with your finger moving counterclockwise.)
3. *The short stick is made down the right side of the circle.*

Constructing the Exercise Sheets for Tracing and Writing Activities.

You will need to prepare two exercise sheets for each lesson, one for the capital (see illustration page 28) and one for the lower case version of each letter (see illustration page 33). These will all be constructed using exactly the same format. Each will have four rows, the first entirely filled with letters to be traced, the second containing one letter at the beginning and one in the middle of the row, and the final two rows with only one letter at the beginning.

You may wish to construct all your exercise sheets at one time, keeping them in the tablet or in a folder for easy referral. Make sure that you construct the letters carefully according to the guidelines in the alphabet chart. Also, don't forget to place the numbers and arrows on the first letter of the first row. (If the numbers and arrows prove confusing, just show the child where to start.) Should you ever feel more practice is needed for any particular letter, by all means make up another exercise sheet on the spot and have your child complete it. Also whenever the child watches you form the letters, be sure to use the same sequence of strokes recommended in the alphabet chart.

Structured Writing Exercise Sheets

You will remember that the structured writing activities are designed only for the child who does not learn how to print a letter within the routine tracing, writing, memorization, and practice framework. Illustrated at the end of the chapter are the essential elements needed to construct all structured writing exercise sheets which you may or may not need while teaching the remaining lessons in this chapter. If you do use them, follow these guidelines:

1. Make the exercise sheet exactly as described on page 29-30 and shown in the illustration on page 30.

2. Make sure the child always observes the correct starting point and the correct sequence of strokes. This applies even when part of the letter is reproduced. In **T**, for example, when the child is asked to complete a partial figure, he will first trace over the vertical line already there before supplying the horizontal line on top.

3. Explain what the dots, arrows, and numbers represent on the first letter and allow the child to refer back to it whenever he wishes. The dot indicates where to put the pencil when starting.

4. Use guidewords. Begin by repeating them yourself, then say them with the child toward the eventual goal of enabling him to repeat them on his own as he prints the letter. Guide words may be dropped once the sequence of strokes has been memorized.

5. Allow as much practice as needed. If more exercise sheets are called for, supply them.

6. Be positive. If your child needs the structured writing activities, it means that printing is difficult for him at this stage in his development. Do everything possible to encourage him and to keep writing from becoming an aversive experience.

Review

Some form of review should be instituted every third or fourth lesson, depending upon individual needs. These activities can be extremely simple. Be sure to make your exercises large enough for the child to read comfortably.

1. Prepare a tablet page so that each row starts with one of the letter formations studied to that point. Have the child fill in the rows with the letters in question. You may conduct this activity using the memorization procedure instead.

2. Dictate the letters which have been studied and have the child write both the capital and lower case formations. If trouble is encountered for any letter, repeat part of the formal lesson as indicated. (A fun variation of this activity involves mixing up the letter cards and placing them face down on the desk or table. The child then hands the parent one without looking, the parent reads it, and the child writes both capital

and lower case forms. The card is turned over and, if the letter is correctly drawn, the child keeps the card. If not, it is mixed back into the stack. The game ends when all letter cards belong to the child.)

3. Prepare an exercise sheet like the one below and have the child connect the two forms of each letter with a line.

T	i
L	t
I	e
F	l
E	o
O	f

4. Present an answer sheet containing letters already studied like the one below:

Tt	Ll	Ii	Oo	_____
Ll	Oo	Ee	Ii	_____
Ff	Tt	Oo	Ee	_____
Ee	Tt	Ff	Oo	_____
Ff	Ll	Oo	Tt	_____
Oo	Ii	Tt	Ee	_____

Now read one letter for each row, telling the child to: *Circle the letter as I say it, then write it in the blank.*

Ll	Ff	Ii	Ee	Tt	Oo

5. Copy the capital and small letters to be reviewed with a blank between them. Cover the small letters with a folded piece of paper or index card, then have the child look at each capital letter and write the lower case counterpart in the blank. He may then slide the folded paper down one line to expose the lower case letter and see if he was correct.

F	_____	f
A	_____	a
L	_____	l
N	_____	n
I	_____	i
W	_____	w
H	_____	h
M	_____	m
O	_____	o
E	_____	e
V	_____	v
T	_____	t

(The activity can be repeated on another occasion to review upper case letters by simply reversing the columns.)

These are only a small sample of the many ways you can help your child review what he has learned up to a particular point. Feel free to improvise. Any activity in which letters need to be written will be effective.

Adding Meaning

The child must be made to realize, as soon as possible that writing is a way of communicating meaning. It is not enough to tell him; he must see it for himself.

Reading to him will help him make this connection, especially if you point out words and letters as you go. Similarly, his reading instruction will help him see the relationship as well, but you mustn't forget that the association between typeset letters and the ones he is learning to print may not be as obvious to a child as it is to an adult. Similarly, the prose in books has very little in common with the way a child talks and the things he wishes to say.

What you are going to have to do, therefore, is to demonstrate that the letters he is learning to print can be used to *communicate meaning*. Beginning in Lesson 7 you will routinely add a set of activities at the end of the lesson which do just that. In addition, they will begin the process of teaching your child some of the rudimentary principles of capitalization and spacing between words.

The actual words and sentences which will be used in the twenty lessons incorporating the "Adding Meaning" activities follow:

LESSON 7. Mom, Me
LESSON 8. The Hill
LESSON 9. The Hen
LESSON 10. Tall Man, The Hat
LESSON 11. TV
LESSON 12. We
LESSON 13. The Zoo
LESSON 14. The Toy
LESSON 15. Kite
LESSON 16. A Boy
LESSON 17. My Dad (Daddy)
LESSON 18. Jet
LESSON 19. My Pal
LESSON 20. Red Bird
LESSON 21. The Car
LESSON 22. A Big Girl
LESSON 23. Up

LESSON 24. **The Queen is Here**
LESSON 25. **It is Summer**
LESSON 26. **EXIT**

Although these "Adding Meaning" exercises are only one of several activities which go into the teaching of each lesson, they should be attacked with a great deal of vigor and enthusiasm. Suggest to the child that he start writing a book of his own. Tell him that for each lesson he will get to draw a picture and give it a title.

Children love the idea of making their own books. Enlist other members of the family to look at and compliment each page as it is added. Hang especially good efforts in a prominent place in the home before entering them in the book. In other words, do everything you can think of to make this initial writing foray a rewarding experience.

For each given lesson you will generally follow these steps:

1. Have the child draw a picture relevant to the words listed above;
2. Present these words to him on individual word cards you have printed;
3. Have him copy the words on a tablet page;
4. Cut out the best efforts and paste them on the top or bottom of the picture; and
5. Place the picture in the child's personal book.

To illustrate this process, let's examine how the "Adding Meaning" section of Lesson 7 might be taught. Following the practice and review activities in Part III you would have the child draw a picture of his mother and himself. Make up two word cards containing "Mom" and "Me" and present them to the child while reading and spelling the words aloud. Point to each letter as you spell the words; then have the child point to the letters and spell with you.

Put the word cards aside and take out a pencil and tablet page. Write "Mom" and "Me" on the top line leaving plenty of space between them. Say:

Write "Mom" just below where it says "Mom", and "Me" just below where "Me" is written.

Show where you want this done on the page and have all the lines below the first filled in in the same way. (Make sure the child leaves ample space between words.)

Praise these first efforts lavishly. Offer positive suggestions and guidance by looking at each word on the completed page and pointing out the details that are among the child's best efforts. Say things such as, "Look how nice this 'M' looks" or "The word 'Me' is really done well here." Remember not to be overly critical. Beginners' writing almost always looks awkward, disproportionate, and shaky.

Pick out the best attempts at "Mom" and "Me" and cut them out (or draw a rectangle around each and have the child cut them out) and paste them together under the child's pictures. Don't do this routinely. Make a major production out of it! After all, this is the first page of his book. (He may prefer to have his picture hung up for everyone in the family to see first.) Explain that what he has written is called a title. If he doesn't know what a title is, pull out some story books and point out how titles give stories or pictures a name.

Use a binder, loose leaf notebook, or construct something yourselves to keep the "Adding Meaning" activities and other things your child writes together. Let him decorate the cover and show off his book to family members and friends. There are no rules; just use your child's imagination, your own ideas, and have a good time!

All the "Adding Meaning" activities can basically be taught in this same manner. Do try to add some small unique touch to each, something that will be especially relevant to your child's personal experiences. For "The Hill" in Lesson 8, for example, suggest that he draw a hill that he has seen or one that would be fun to climb. For "Tall Man" and "The Hat" suggest someone he knows who is tall (most adults will seem so to a child) and a hat that person might wear. For "The Zoo" you might have pictures of animals cut from magazines and newspapers and combined into a collage. Some titles like "Red Bird" and "Up" allow a great deal of creative expression in the drawing of a suitable picture. Lessons 24 and 25 introduce the child to copying complete sentences, but since they are titles, they abide by different punctuation rules which need not be mentioned now. For Lesson 26 you might have him make up EXIT signs and place them at appropriate places in the house.

Let us repeat. There are no rules as to how this activity has to be taught. Furthermore, there is no reason why you must be limited to the words and sentences we have chosen. Pick additional ones if you like; just remember to use only letters that have been introduced and to keep the words and sentences short and simple.

Evaluating the Results of Your Teaching

You will probably have an accurate idea of how well your child prints the alphabet by the end of the last lesson. It is a good idea to administer the printing "test" discussed at the beginning of this chapter anyway. This is done by simply asking your child to print the capital and lower case letters as you dictate them. By carefully examining the results you can determine whether or not more work on certain letters is required. For the school-aged child you should examine whether the letters are of proportionate height and size, whether spacing is adequate, and whether all letters rest on the baseline. Comparing it to the child's performance prior to your beginning the chapter (if you administered the test then) should also prove quite interesting.

In the final analysis you will have to make the decision yourself as to whether or not to reteach certain lessons. Just remember that no one prints perfectly and that almost all children improve naturally with both practice and age. The best rule of thumb is to go on to the other writing activities in this book if the child can make a legible approximation of a letter. There is no reason why you cannot intersperse reviews of these lessons throughout your other teaching activities. If the child completely fails in an attempt to produce a commonly occurring letter, you should continue to teach the relevant lesson at the same time you engage in other activities.

Whatever you do, don't attach too much significance to your child's failure to learn as quickly as you think he should. There are no quick and easy solutions. Be patient. Keep giving him practice. If he is a young preschooler, teaching a few letters now will make learning the rest easier later on. If the child is of school age, he may have less difficulty with cursive writing and can still learn to express himself via the typewriter. Give your child all the time he needs to learn. Above all, never make him feel he has failed for that is the fastest way to discourage learning itself. All children are learners. Some just require more time for some things.

OUTLINE FOR STRUCTURED WRITING EXERCISES

V W Z Y K

V W Z Y K

V V Z V F

V Z V

B D J P R

R D J P R

P D J P P

P P J F P

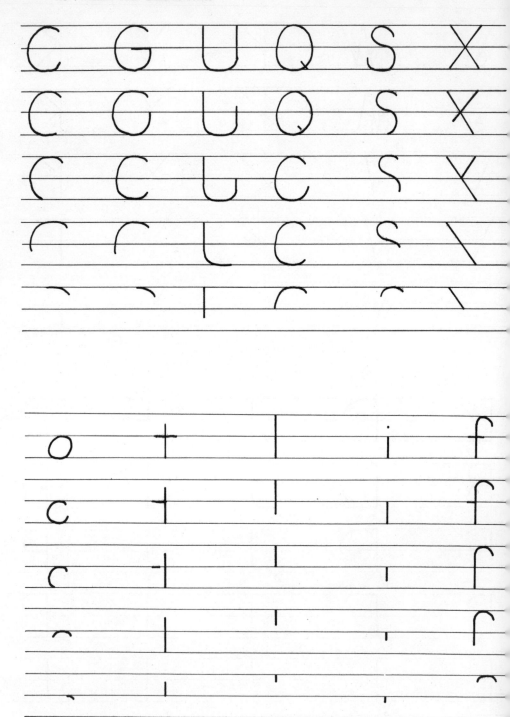

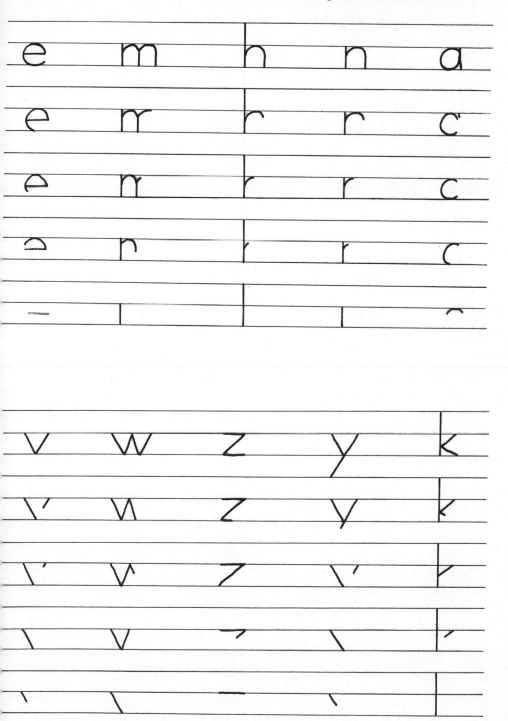

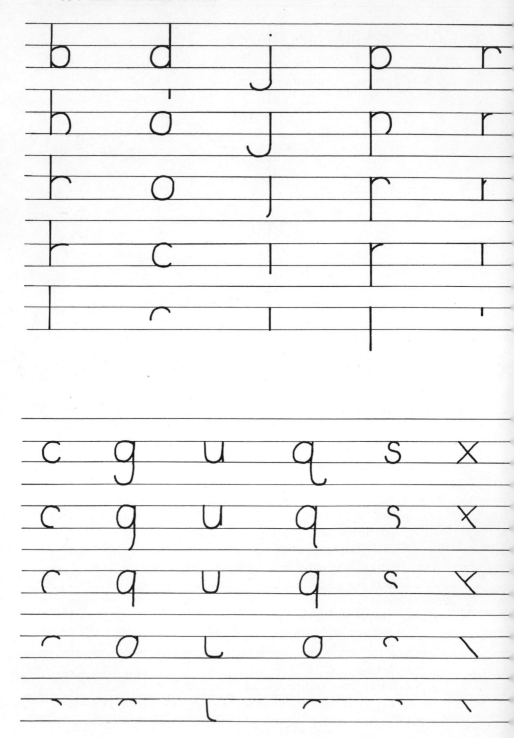

Special Problems Related to Learning to Print

Although it is not well recognized, handwriting plays an important part in overall academic success. Some difficulty is to be expected when the child first begins to print, but problems which show no improvement over time (persisting into the second and third grades) or whose severity hinders early learning experiences warrant careful monitoring. Before a problem, no matter how small, can be corrected it must be identified and its nature understood. Here are some of the more common difficulties that may be normally encountered in the young learner but should disappear with experience and maturity:

1. **Sloppiness.** If initial performance is acceptable and sloppiness sets in later, calling attention to substandard performance as soon as the child begins to waver usually suffices. Be careful however! Genuine difficulties sometime appear as sloppiness and go unrecognized for years.

2. **Reversals.** Differences between similar looking letters (**b/d, n/u, p/q**) are not readily perceived.

3. **Ordering.** The ordering of letters is not perceived, such as **on/no.**

4. **Size and position.** When copying, difficulty may be encountered in making letters the correct size or "sitting" them on the lines of the page. Letters may seem to float and slant down the page; words may be broken up; some sentences may even start on the right side of the page and work toward the left.

5. **Odd sequence of strokes.** Letters, even when copied correctly, may be formed in odd ways. (Strokes on some letters may be written in an unconventional order, such as the "stick" on the lower-case **a** being written prior to the "circle". Some letters may even be formed differently each time they are copied.)

6. **Spacing.** Intervals between letters or words may be too great or small giving the writing an extremely "bunched" look, often making it difficult to determine where one word starts and another begins.

7. **Capital/lower-case substitutions.** Capital instead of lower-case letters may be used because they are easier to remember.

A child may experience any or all of these difficulties without there being any real cause for alarm. It is the severity and the persistence of the problem in question which dictates whether or not special steps need be taken. If you decide some action is warranted *the first step should always be a consultation with your pediatrician who may then refer you to other specialists*. The more common reversals (mentioned above), for example, sometimes persist as late as the third grade without any lasting effect, yet these same problems can extend to other letters (such as **g, k, a,** and **r**) and may be correlated with left to right progression problems in reading, writing, and other non-academic phases of the child's life.

If special therapy in the form of concentrated, systematic teaching is warranted, the techniques and activities presented in this and later chapters can be brought directly to bear on the child's specific problems. You must remember, however, that learning must be an *enjoyable, low pressure, no-lose proposition* for the child or it will not occur. Keep your correctional lessons short and light. You are in no real hurry and the next chapter will show you how to teach your child to express himself in writing through means other than printing.

3

The First Steps in Writing

You have chosen to read this book because you want to teach your child to write. This chapter will show you how to begin to do just that. It can be used with the school age child or with the very young child who has not yet been formally introduced to the process, who may not yet know how to form all the letters, and who needs the transition from oral to written expression divided into as many small steps as possible. All the strategies and activities can be adjusted to the level of the child's expertise.

If you judge the activities presented to be too elementary for your child, then by all means proceed to Chapter Four. Be warned, however, that learning to write is not a quick, easy process. Children just do not begin writing fluently after a few short lessons any more than they learn to talk that way. If you have any doubts about how advanced your child really is, err on the side of conservatism: try some of these activities and see what happens. It will be obvious to you if they are too elementary.

If you have begun to teach your child to read, the slowness with which writing skills are attained may be frustrating. It is much easier to *see* progress in a subject like reading which is composed of a multitude of small learning steps. To be an effective writing teacher, however, you must first learn to be patient. If you do, and if you afford ample practice, then your child will learn to write just as surely as he learned to talk.

Writing, A Language Process

Nothing can prepare a child for writing better than an environment in which language development is actively promoted. We say actively because all parents teach their children to speak with little conscious effort. It is the deliberate verbal exchange between parent and child that is of utmost importance. Children who are seen but not heard do not become articulate speakers, and it is your child's speech that will be reflected in his writing. Listening to what he has to say, questioning him, getting him to think, providing a good language model yourself, are the things that make verbal exchange deliberate.

Providing the child with a rich background of experiences on which to draw, and discussing those experiences with him is one of the most important factors in language development. Reading to the child is also unparalleled as a forum for engaging in the exchange of ideas and opinions, exercising listening skills, expanding the imagination, and developing appreciation for print. All these things will make your child a better writer. Continue to do them.

Writing versus Penmanship

As we stated in the first chapter, written expression is not synonymous with letter formation. Penmanship is only a writing tool, a means to an end like the typewriter or the dictaphone. Children can learn to express themselves in writing long before they have attained any true facility in forming the letters of the alphabet *if* someone takes the time to print for them, type for them, or to spell out words as the child types.

Because the classroom teacher cannot afford the time necessary for this, many children do not learn to write as well as they might in the public schools. It is not a conventional approach, but it is the best way to encourage children to begin to write early. To argue that it is not really the child who does the writing in these circumstances makes no more sense than to say the blind John Milton was not really the author of *Paradise Lost* because he dictated it to his daughters.

At any rate, we do not require that your child master thoroughly the printing skills presented in Chapter Two before he learns to write. To do so would waste precious time, time which can never really be replaced. Instead, we suggest that you begin working through the activities presented in this and the next chapter *at the same time* you teach the printing lessons.

You will, of course, encourage your child to print what he writes whenever feasible. The truth of the matter is, however, that even when the letters can be formed quite adequately, printing passages of any length will continue to be a laborious process for some time to come. Forcing the child to do all his own printing would make written expression laborious as well, and that is a state of affairs that should be avoided at all costs. The child must enjoy writing if he is going to practice enough to become good at it, and the only way that is going to happen is for you to help share in the task of writing down what is created. This means that the child dictates what he wants to write and you write it for him. Gradually, the student will be weaned away from sole dependence on you by first beginning to copy or type what you print, and then later branching out on his own.

The Typewriter. Until handwriting is no longer a problem, the typewriter is a godsend for young authors. Using the index finger, many children find typing less cumbersome and more exciting than printing, once they are taught the rudiments of paper installation, carriage control, and spacing.

If you have any doubts about the economic wisdom of investing in a child's typewriter, forget them. Toy typewriters that function quite adequately are inexpensive. You don't need anything fancy. Ask around and you may even discover an old leviathan sitting unused in a friend's attic. If it types, it's good enough. Just avoid electric typewriters for they allow mistakes to be made too easily.

A final argument for procuring a typewriter, and perhaps the best one, is that children love playing with them. If you are like most parents, you spend a lot more money than the price of a typewriter on flashy toys that don't last and are not the least bit educational. With a typewriter, the child plays with letters and words, and that is really what writing is all about.

Typesetting. Another writing strategy to be used in addition to (or in lieu of) the typewriter is typesetting. Cut out small 1″ × 1″ pieces of index cards to serve as "letter squares." Print the capital letters on one side, their lower case counterparts on the other. (Another option is to use an old Scrabble set and print the lower case letter in pen on the blank side of each square.) In any case place the letters (you will need several of each) alphabetically in some sort of compartments (for example, an empty candy box that contained plastic dividers, or a few egg cartons) writing the letter in the bottom of each compartment so the child can maintain the alphabetical order. You now have the makings of a nonmechanical typewriter!

The next step, of course, is for the child to combine the letters together to make words. They can simply be laid down on a flat surface, but it is nice to insert them in slots so final products don't blow away at the slightest sneeze. One possibility is to paste a few rows of the triangular slots used in picture albums on a piece of cardboard. The child puts the bottom corners of the letter squares in the picture holders, skipping a couple to space between words. Another option is to fold up the bottom of a long index card ¼″ or so to serve as a tray for holding the letter squares. If you are using Scrabble chips, the Scrabble trays make excellent holders.

Commercial letter squares are also available in which one side of the letter is sticky and can be placed on a sheet of paper. If you decide to employ this strategy, be sure to "typeset" so that the words will be reasonably straight.

While in many ways typesetting is not as satisfactory as typing, it is cheaper, allows more physical manipulation of letters, and gradually teaches alphabetical order. There is, in fact, no reason why both aids can't be employed to add variety to the writing process.

Spelling

Another reason to help your child put his words on paper is that although it normally takes some time for him to learn to form his letters easily, it will take him even longer to combine those letters into words. Learning to spell can, like learning to print, take a long time, and, like printing, spelling is only a tool which need not be perfected in order for self-expression to take place. In fact, the child who is required to attempt to spell every word he wants to write will be much less adventuresome in what he produces. We therefore recommend that spelling be taught only after the child has become comfortable expressing himself in writing as taught in this chapter. In the meantime, let him write words as they sound or encourage him to ask you how to spell words.

Materials For Getting Started

One of the best ways to encourage your child to begin to write is to make sure he has an abundance of personal writing materials available at all times. For some children, in fact, this is practically all that is needed, coupled with a little help, encouragement, and guidance from an interested adult. For most, however, more structured teaching will be required as discussed in subsequent portions of this and the next chapter. Here are materials you might consider, some of which will be used in the suggested activities:

1. **Lined Tablet Paper.** As employed in Chapter Two.
2. **Primary Story Paper.** Similar to tablet paper except space is left at the top of each page to permit a picture to be drawn.
3. **Scrap Paper.** This can include practically anything: backs of junk mail, typing paper, pieces cut from bags, cardboard, and so forth.
4. **Primary Pencils.**
5. **Pencil Sharpener.** (optional) Both useful and a delight for many children.
6. **Alphabet Strip.** See Chapter Two, page 24.
7. **Crayons.**
8. **Colored Pencils.** (optional)
9. **Pens.** (optional) Pens have an unexplained fascination for children, especially those with different colored inks. If you decide to allow their use, make sure that they contain water soluable ink.
10. **Scissors, Paste, Rulers,** (*paint*, optional).
11. **Old Magazines.** To be used as sources of pictures to be cut out and traced. The more you have the better so don't hesitate to ask friends to collect them for you.
12. **Index Cards.** Of various sizes.
13. **File Card Box.** To house the index cards. This may include an actual filing box (plastic ones are available quite cheaply) or a simple cardboard container such as a greeting card box.

14. **Boxes and/or Folders.** For storing materials.
15. **Typewriter.** (optional) Either a toy or very inexpensive surplus model and/or *Letter Squares.*
16. **Chalk Board.** (optional) While not essential, many children enjoy practicing their writing on a chalk board. Be aware, however, that forming letters on a vertical surface is somewhat different than on a horizontal piece of paper and that some special instruction may be required. A small board is well worth the money if it can stimulate writing output. It can be used, in a number of ways from copying words to leaving messages or questions.
17. **Bulletin Board.** (optional) This aid can be used by the entire family for a number of writing related purposes.
18. **Desk or Table with Chair.** These should be the right height to allow the child to work comfortably. Many children prefer to write on the floor, which is fine. For homework assignments, however, a desk is preferable. Whatever his individual tastes, however, you will probably find that your child likes to work where his parents write, read, sew, or do other quiet work. Few children enjoy working alone until they are truly comfortable with the task at hand.
19. **Picture Dictionary.** (optional) Several options are available commercially. These books serve several purposes: they introduce the concept and use of a dictionary, foster learning alphabetical order, serve as a spelling reference, yield ideas for stories via their colorful pictures, help teach a basic reading vocabulary, and simply provide an interesting picture book for leisure time enjoyment. Two popular choices are:
The Cat in the Hat Beginner's Book Dictionary by P. D. Eastman (New York: Beginner Books, Random House, 1964). This dictionary for beginning readers explains words through simple sentence examples and pictures by Dr. Seuss.
The Charlie Brown Dictionary compiled by Charles M. Schulz (Cleveland: World Books, 1973). This picture dictionary is for slightly older children in kindergarten through third grade. It is illustrated with over 800 cartoons from the popular *Peanuts* comic series and its 2400 entries reflects the language that children speak and hear.

Activities for Using the Materials

Once you have supplied the basic raw materials, it is time to begin systematically teaching your child to express himself in writing. This will be done through a series of activities gradually increasing in sophistication.

ACTIVITY #1.
Writing Titles

If you read to your child he probably already has a good concept of what titles are. Since composing them is going to be his first writing assignment, however, you should explain that titles are really names which describe what a story or picture is all about. He is familiar with names, maybe even having learned to print his own by now, and will experience little difficulty making the association.

Once this is done, leaf through a story book or magazine pointing out the titles. Write a few down showing him how the first, the last, and each important word begins with a capital letter, and how they are written in the middle of the top line on the page. Short, unimportant words found in the middle, such as "the," "and," "in," "a," and "of," are not capitalized. Copy examples, such as the ones below, reading them to the child, pointing out which words are capitalized, and then asking what each story must be about based on the title:

> A Bird in the House
> The Dog and the Cat
> The Halloween Party
> A Baby Chick

Multiple-Choice Titles. Now that the child has a general idea of what titles are, this activity will help him learn to choose titles. Paste a picture on a piece of paper and write two or three titles underneath. After discussing the picture, read the different choices while the child looks on, then ask him to circle the one which best describes the story in the picture. Be sure to ask why he picked the one he did and why it was better than the other alternatives. As an example, if the picture showed a family looking at a new car in a showroom, the title choices might be:

Buying a New Car
A Ride in the Country
The Swimming Party

Once some confidence is obtained with this activity, the child should be ready to graduate to suggesting titles on his own.

Titling the Child's Own Pictures. As discussed in Chapter Two you should encourage your child to draw his own pictures on a regular basis, both from the standpoint of developing fine motor skills and as a means of self-expression. These experiences can now be used for additional practice in composing titles. Most children have no difficulty at all labeling their own artwork, and usually enjoy copying the titles themselves (by printing, typing, or typesetting). Assembling the titled illustrations in a loose-leaf notebook with the child listed as author is an additional incentive.

Collect several pictures showing people and/or animals, mount each on a page of lined tablet paper with plenty of room at the top, and show one to the child. Ask what is happening in the picture. If necessary, bring out the story in the picture by such questions as:

1. *Who (what) is in the picture?*
2. *Where are they?*
3. *What are they doing?*
4. *Do you think these people know each other?* (for example, Mother and children)
5. *What do you think they will do next?*

Following the discussion, say:

Now that you know so much about the picture, can you name it?

Write the title at the top of the tablet page, (or spell the words for the child to print), then have him read it.

Continue this activity to give the child practice at creating titles. Print or spell for him whenever necessary.

Writing Story Titles Reading to your child also provides an excellent opportunity for writing titles. To take advantage of it, don't give away the title of the story you are reading or mention what it's about. Instead, say that you want him to come up with a title.

Below is a passage we read to a group of children just beginning the second grade before asking them to compose a name for the story:

> Jim and Betty were playing in the yard. All at once Jim stopped playing. He put his fingers to his lips to show Betty to be still. Betty stopped playing and looked where Jim was pointing. Then she knew what Jim saw. She saw something with long ears, a short tail that looked like a cotton ball, and a nose that moved to show its excitement. It had whiskers sticking out on each side of its nose.

Since the children involved could already print, we had them print their own titles and sign their own names. (If your child is not yet this advanced, you will, of course, write what he says.) Here is what we got:

> Rabbit
> A rabbet
> "the Rabbit"
> "The Rabbit"
> "Rabbit"
> "the little rabbit"
> I Rabbet for Laem and Baey

As you can see, all of the children came up with a suitable title for the passage. Some of the spelling and capitalization could be improved, and one student reversed the capital J. Since the purpose of the lesson was to write a title for a story obviously about a rabbit, however, we considered the exercise quite successful. It is our belief that the types of spelling, printing, and punctuation errors exhibited would be best addressed at another time unless a particular child was extremely confident in his writing. Read the above story to your child and see what title he suggests.

Here is another story to entitle. Read it to the child; then read the three choices of titles and ask him to choose the best one.

I am made of many bright colors. Sometimes I am either red, yellow, blue, or some other color. I may even have beautiful flowers or checks of different colors. I close when not in use, open up when needed. I make a dark day bright and keep my owner dry. Sometimes I keep your friend dry too. Choose my title.

An Umbrella
A Walk with a Friend
A Dark Day

This next story is slightly more difficult. If the child cannot come up with a title on his own, provide a choice of three as in the previous story.

John asked all his friends to come to his house after school. When they arrived John's mother gave each of them a funny hat to wear. They put these on and looked happy and funny.

They played lots of games and some of them won prizes. When they were tired of playing, John's Mother invited them into the dining room.

Each child found his name at a place at the table. Here were some funny little baskets with nuts and candy. John's Mother brought in the cake. There were seven lighted candles, but John blew all of them out. Then she gave each child a piece of cake and a dish of ice cream.

Name the story.

Expanding the Language in Titles. Once the child begins to become comfortable writing titles, you should start encouraging the use of more specific, descriptive language. Instead of titling a picture "The Sky," for example, suggest that its color be incorporated, such as "The Blue Sky." Later, encourage more description, such as "The Blue Sky with Clouds." Then expand even more upon the clouds with "The Blue Sky with Big Fluffy White Clouds." Try to point out how much more each word tells the reader. If the child encounters trouble with this exercise, provide help in the form of questions: "What color is the sky?" "Is it big or little?" "Can anything be seen in the sky?"

Occasionally the child will write a sentence in this way. When that happens, tell him: *Good. This tells more than a title so we'll write it as a sentence.* Copy his sentence below the story or picture as a caption, pointing out that a sentence expresses a whole thought, begins with a capital letter and ends with a period. Sentences need not be taught yet, but whenever one is constructed, show its correct written form.

ACTIVITY #2
Writing Lists and Notes

Lists are an everyday writing activity in which the novice writer can easily participate. When making up the grocery list, ask the child to help figure out what is needed and add an item.

Notes are also commonly written in many households. If one parent leaves word that he is going somewhere with the child, allow the child to sign his name even if he can't read the note himself.

Before the child becomes a full participant in these activities he can learn how essential writing is to everyday communications. Involving him whenever possible, even in a small way, is an important first step.

ACTIVITY #3
Constructing a Picture Dictionary

There are times when your child will want to write on his own without requesting help from an adult. For these occasions, having a spelling reference such as a picture dictionary available is a big help. As excellent as the commercial versions discussed earlier are, there are definite advantages in having a child construct his own.

In the first place, his personal dictionary will be stocked with words in his own vocabulary, words which he is most likely to want to use when writing. Secondly, the process of constructing the dictionary, of writing the words, selecting pictures, and alphabetizing them is an extremely valuable activity in and of itself. Finally, and perhaps most importantly, children derive tremendous satisfaction in compiling permanent, useful records of their achievement both for their own and others' appreciation.

To construct a picture dictionary all you need do is write a word your child asks about or uses frequently on a large index card (for example, 6″ × 8″). Next, select an appropriate picture, or have one drawn, and paste it below the word. File the finished product in a box having alphabetical dividers (these are available in most office supply stores) and you are in business.

Putting together a picture dictionary can be a gradual process or a regular daily activity. It should be reviewed periodically with the child reading you the entries. It should also be used extensively.

If your child asks how to spell a word in his dictionary, make sure you help him look it up instead of supplying it as you do other words.

Those parents using our program to teach their children to read will notice a similarity between the picture dictionary and the Word Box, which serves as a permanent record of all the words that can be read. If your child does have a Word Box, then it should definitely be used as a spelling guide now as well.

Don't neglect to use pictures drawn by the child. Drawing is an excellent means of self-expression and fine motor development. It also doesn't matter if you are not particularly impressed with the quality of an illustration as long as it is recognizable to the artist.

WRITING AS A CONTINUOUS PROCESS

Unlike the other basic skills, reading and arithmetic, writing is not given to easy compartmentalization, step-by-step lesson plans, or competency tests that can tell you exactly when a skill has been mastered through a correct or incorrect response to a question. In many ways this characteristic makes writing a more interesting subject to teach (and to learn). You don't necessarily have to wait until one phase has been mastered before moving on to the next; thus, if you sense interest flagging on one set of activities, you can introduce another and either work on both simultaneously, or simply leave the first for a better time. The most important thing to remember in teaching writing is to keep the child practicing. Practice may not make perfect, but it certainly improves.

The next chapter is given over primarily to teaching the child to write more expansively, to construct and combine grammatically complete sentences into different types of prose. We do not expect you to wait until your child's titles approach an art form before tackling stories any more than we wanted you to wait until he printed perfectly to attempt this chapter. Feel free to take any direction at any pace your child's individual skills, interests, and circumstances dictate. There are no rules in teaching writing save to write, write, and write.

4
Writing

Now the fun begins. Your child's first tentative steps toward written communication are behind him. He is gradually growing more confident in his ability to express himself, whether through dictation or by actually doing his own printing. He is, in other words, ready to learn to write.

All the topics in this book are rewarding to teach, but you will probably find this chapter the most interesting. Unlike the others, it has no real end, other than that distant point at which either your child's skills outstrip yours or he becomes capable of teaching himself.

There are, of course, skills chapters still to be taught, such as: handwriting, sentence construction, spelling, and grammatical concepts without whose mastery true writing potential cannot be realized. By and large, however, the lessons in these chapters (Five through Nine) should be separated from the activities presented here.

What we suggest you do for now, therefore, is to separate writing *skills* from the writing process dealt with in this chapter as much as possible. Skills are reducible to small steps with right and wrong answers involving little ego investment. They can be taught through specific, brief lessons which are best interspersed with the writing activities of this chapter. *You will, therefore, use the child's areas of weakness in writing to devise appropriate skills lessons as found in the remaining chapters.* The child, however, need not be aware that you are analyzing his writing for these weaknesses.

This is not to say that these skills lessons will never be integrated into the creative process. Gradually, as your child grows more and more confident in his ability to express himself in writing, you can point out more and more ways a composition could be improved. Some children, in fact, have so much ingrained confidence that this can be done from the beginning, just as some parents are so skillful and tactful that the problems we fear can never arise. If there is any doubt at all, however, we suggest that you exercise extreme caution.

We recommend that you treat this chapter as a series of entertaining activities to engage in as often as possible. By interspersing them with the later skills lessons on a regular basis, we predict you will find the process rewarding on two levels. As a parent you will enjoy seeing your child develop crucial skills, which will be increasingly useful throughout his life. As a teacher you will appreciate the luxury of a subject whose activities do not have to be judged, only enjoyed.

General Guidelines for Teaching this Chapter

1. **Age.** The activities in this chapter become progressively more advanced. The simplest could be used by beginning readers while the majority can be used throughout the elementary school years.

2. **Order and rate of progress.** The activities presented earlier in the chapter are easier, and thus more appropriate for very young and beginning writers than those presented later. This certainly does not mean, however, that you should progress through the chapter activity-by-activity, idea-by-idea. Feel free to skip around, varying your writing assignments to meet the special interests and needs of your child.

There is no set timetable for completion. Nowhere do individual differences manifest themselves more prominently than in writing; the important thing is to simply give your child as many opportunities to practice as possible.

3. **Printing.** Although it is not absolutely essential that your

child print everything he composes in this chapter, you should continue to encourage him to take on more and more responsibility in this regard. In other words, although it is permissable for you to print his dictation part of the time, try to gradually wean him away from total dependency. One interesting twist to this process is to furnish the child with an uncomplicated (and inexpensive) tape recorder and allow him to dictate to it. Once he learns how to erase and edit what he has said, he will be well on the way to achieving independence.

4. **Spelling.** Spelling lessons should not begin before the child is reading near an early second grade level. Until then you must permit a good deal of leeway and continue to provide help. In any case, remember to encourage the sounding out of words when possible as well as the use of aids like the picture dictionaries and word box. If in your judgment your child is ready for spelling lessons, then intersperse the activities from Chapter Six between the writing sessions.

5. **Editing.** Reading over the composition, erasing words, and rewriting sections that don't sound right should be considered an integral part of the writing. We have discussed this in some detail under Activity #11 below, but in the meantime, *always* have your child read his work aloud prior to considering it complete. Show your pleasure in what he has expressed. Encourage him to change anything he doesn't like, ask you about words that look misspelled, and so forth. Don't worry about sloppiness; just strive to help him turn out the best work possible.

6. **Criticism.** We don't believe most young children are ready for systematic critiques of their writing efforts. This is not to say that you can't offer suggestions occasionally. We will show you how to draw out ideas and make suggestions subtly through questions. Generally speaking, however, your chief objective at this point is to encourage your child to write by teaching him to enjoy it. (As discussed later, the rules for report writing are a little different.)

7. **Saving the child's writing.** The child's writing should be systematically saved for a number of reasons. If placed in a special notebook with the author's name on the cover, it will be a source of pride and incentive for continued writing that can be shared with family and friends. If saved over a considerable period of time, it can help you assess rate of progress. Finally, we will show you in later chapters how individual writings can be made into remedial exercises to help later on with skill development. (For example,

misspelled words can be identified for future lessons, un-grammatical sentences presented for correction, and so forth.)

8. **Reading to your child.** Reading to your child *will* help him learn to write. Although most children won't learn to write solely through reading or being read to, seeing and hearing how other writers communicate can eventually have an effect upon writing. Read to your child regularly and encourage him to read on his own.

9. **Provide a model.** Children are born imitators. The best way to instill the importance of writing is to make it an integral part of *your* lifestyle. Be seen making out grocery lists, leaving notes to family members, writing letters, and so forth. Involve children in the process whenever possible.

10. **Providing an audience.** Every type of writing discussed in this chapter (with the exception of diaries) assumes an audience. People write to communicate with other people. If you do not provide an attentive, interested ear, the child will not believe that his writing is of real value. Always show interest in hearing a composition as soon as it is written. Parental interest and apprecia-tion are most important for a beginning writer to have on his side. The child must feel that what he has produced is important and special. Occasionally, the child might enjoy writing for an apprecia-tive recipient other than his parent, such as a grandparent, sibling, or friend.

The First Step: Getting the Child to Write Stories

Story writing, and by that we mean anything longer than one sentence, can begin in the same way as writing titles. The subject matter can be absolutely anything that interests your child: an experience, a description of a place or thing, a biography or autobiography, fact or fiction.

Chances are the first story will be dictated spontaneously as an outgrowth of the activities in Chapter Three. If not, several scenarios follow, any one of which is quite acceptable. Be sure to write down exactly what is dictated, have the entire story read back to you, and be very positive regardless of your opinion concerning its true literary merits. (If the story comes early in your child's reading career *you* should read it aloud first as the child looks on.) Remember also that early writing can often be improved by (1) discussing what is to be written first to help thoughts jell, (2) encouraging the expression of *feelings* and *opinions* that will make the story more interesting, and (3) determining the story's audience (you, for example, your spouse, a sibling, friend, or the child himself).

1. **From a title.** By the end of Chapter Three you were already encouraging more elaborate, descriptive titles. This process can be taken one logical step further by asking the child to tell you anything else about the picture or story. If he has trouble, ask some specific questions and write down the answers.

2. **From a picture.** Select a number of pictures, perhaps some cut from magazines, newspapers, junk mail, or some of the child's own creation. Ask him to select one in turn that he would like to write about. If he has trouble starting a story, allow him to write a title first, then elaborate as above.

3. **Prior to drawing a picture.** Undoubtedly, your child will be very comfortable drawing pictures by now. Usually, as in number two, the picture will serve as the starting point for a story. Sometimes the process can be reversed, however, by suggesting that a story be written about the topic first, before the picture is begun. (Be sure to allow some time for a suitable topic to be chosen.) If this draws a blank, request that the picture's contents be described prior to its creation as you print the description. After this has been completed, the illustration itself can grace the top of the prose description.

4. **After hearing someone else's story.** Hopefully, you are reading regularly *to* your child as a means of facilitating language development, reading ability, and just plain enjoyment. Why not use this process as a means of stimulating writing as well? After an especially well-received story ask the child if he would like to write a similar one involving the same characters or genre (for example, mystery, adventure, and so forth). Don't expect a full-blown short story from this effort; just be thankful for whatever is created.

5. **From an experience.** For the child who needs more stimulation than the above scenarios provide, you can always structure a trip or other activity for the express purpose of providing an idea for a story. Announce your itinerary ahead of time and tell the child that the two of you are going to write about the experience as soon as you get back. Choose any place you please for the excursion: a shopping trip, a visit to the museum, a movie, ball game, or a trip to the zoo. If the child has difficulty writing about the experience

when you return, discuss it with him first, highlighting the interesting and/or amusing things that happened. It will be helpful if you agree upon who the story is being written for and, if some imaginary events find their way into the account, so much the better. If the muses are still silent, you can write a sample story for him, possibly leaving out some of the events you are sure will be remembered so that he can add to your account when encouraged to do so.

6. **Fantasy.** Childhood is a time of unbridled imagination which can serve as unlimited reservoir for writing ideas. Find a topic that intrigues your child, such as "A Trip to the Moon." Discuss how it would feel, what he might find, and what might happen to him. Chances are the writer will have lots to say until it is time to put pencil to paper, at which time he may draw a blank. If that happens, simply review what was said, trying to use his own words as much as possible. Have the child try his hand at writing a fairy tale, tell you what he would do (and what might happen to him) if he had three wishes, and so forth.

The Next Step: Writing for Different Purposes

Once you have solicited a story, no matter how rough, your pre-eminent responsibility is to maintain the momentum. Praise the child's work lavishly, share it with other family members (tipping them off to praise it as well), and place it in a special notebook neatly printed or typed (and perhaps illustrated) with the author's name on the cover. The second thing to do is to encourage your child to write another story as soon as possible, either using the same strategy or one of the actual teaching activities presented below. You may find it helpful at this point to maintain "idea files" such as folders of pictures or titles of potential stories for the child to sift through (with your help) in search of a suitable topic.

Some writers, of course, are more difficult to keep going than others. The following activities, listed by increasing difficulty, can be quite helpful in this regard. Each one also represents a distinct type of writing, to which a child should be given some exposure. If a marked preference is manifested for one activity over another, however, don't hesitate to indulge your child's tastes. Practice is the real key to future writing success.

ACTIVITY #1
Story Reconstruction

Tell the child that you are going to read a story to which he should listen very carefully, because when it's over you want him to write as much of it as he can remember, using any words he chooses.

Read a fairly short story, either of your own making or from one of his books. Next, ask the child to either write or dictate as much of it as he can remember. This particular exercise has the advantage of not taxing your child's possibly undeveloped ability to construct stories on his own while giving him practice in forming sentences and forging them into some sort of narrative.

If the child has difficulty with the process, keep shortening and simplifying the story until it can be remembered. This is not an easy exercise since it calls into play the abilities to listen, comprehend, remember, and reconstruct. The child's version, therefore, may be surprisingly brief, choppy, or different from the original. Don't be discouraged. Practice is what is needed, so simply keep the stories easy until success is achieved. Always read the reconstruction back and praise the effort. Gradually lengthen stories as more proficiency is attained.

To illustrate what seven- and eight-year-old children might produce from this technique, we read the following little story to a group of beginning third graders who were asked to print their own versions. Read it to your child and see what he creates.

THE BACK YARD

Jim and Betty live in a little house with Father and Mother. The little house is just big enough for four people. Jim and Betty like their little house, but most of all, they like the back yard.

The yard is a good place to play. It has a fence and trees and lots of soft grass for running and playing.

The little house is the home of Betty and Jim, but the back yard is the home of many friends.

The big back yard has a little pond. This pond is the home of some of the children's friends, also.

One day as Betty and Jim were playing in the yard, they saw a frog. This frog was big and green. They watched as he sunned himself on the edge of the pond. Then a smaller frog swam up to the edge of the pond and climbed out. This frog sat in the warm spring sunshine by the first frog.

Betty said, "Sh—, here is the Mother Frog."

Jim whispered, "How do you know?"

"That's easy," said Betty softly. "She is not as big as Father Frog."

Jim looked at Betty as if to say, "I doubt that," but he didn't say anything.

Another day the children saw another frog.

"Here is Baby Frog," laughed Betty. "I'll bet its name is Froggie. Now the whole frog family is here."

The children spent many happy days watching Mr. & Mrs. Frog and Froggie as they swam, hopped, and sunned in their back yard.

We allowed the children to either write the story back exactly as they remembered or to write anything they pleased based on it. The first three examples are rather faithful transcriptions; the final three involve the creative flings of born storytellers.

Story #1

Betty and Jim are kids.
Betty and Jim live in
a small house with mother
and father. It has just
enough for four.
But in there own
back yard is fun.
One day they saw a
frog it was big.
Betty and Jim called it
pappa frog. Then they saw
a little frog they called
it mamma frog. They they
saw a small frog the
called it froggie it was
the baby.

Story #2

Jim and Betty live in a little house just big enough for four people. Jim and Betty have a big back yard. But the back yard is the home of many of Jim and Betty's friends. One day while Jim and Betty saw a frog bathing on the side of the pond, soon they saw a bigger green frog jump out of the pond and Betty said now there is a momma and a poppa. They laughed. A few days later Betty saw another little frog then she said now we have a whole family of frogs.

Story #3

THE BACK YARD

Betty and Jim like to play in the
back Yard. and one day Betty and
Jim saw frogs by the pond
they saw an Mother frog and a
father frog and do not for get the
babby frog. and ther are a frog
family Betty and Jim laughed.
Betty and Jim lived with their
Mother and father.

The End

Story #4

The next day Jim and Betty
had for got all about the frogs
because they were going on a
trip. They were going to see Ungle
Roy and Aunt Susie. They
were so excited. Then Aunt
Susie and Ungle Roy took the riding and
Aunt Susie ask how long were
they going to stay. Ungle Roy said
for a week! are they! said Aunt Susie
yes said Ungle Roy. I was just
thinking about those frogs well
said Betty we will find other
frogs to play with yes I guess
so said Jim. When we get home
we will see them once again.
Soon they went home and lived
happily to this day. The End.

Story #5

Evry day they went to see
the frogs after school.
   Then one day in the
   newspaper they were going
   to build a shoping center
   there by the spring.
We can't let that happen said
   Betty. That is the frogs home
and they need a home.
   Then they just rembered
that their grandfather had
a lot that he wanted to sell.
First they called up the
superintendent of the shopping center.
And when they asked he said
yes. Then they called up
   grandfather and he said yes
and the frogs home was saved.

Story #6

then betty and gims mother
called and said to come eat your
dinner, and jim said to betty
what are we going to do with
the grogs if we want to
keep them, and betty said
put it in your pocket gim,
so gim put froggie and the
big dad in one pocket and the
mother frog in the other pocket
so they went to eat their
dinner, and all ob a sudden
something went Ribbit!! and
mother said to her husband
Gorge, stop it Gorge" and he
said I did'nt do nothing
and she said well then
what was it and all
ob a sudden the sudden
little froggie jumped right out
of gims pocket and jumped
down mothers dress and
the mother frog
jumped in fathers soup
and the daddy frog
ran all over the house
knocking things over
and a while later they
caught the frogs and
then Gim and betty explained
it to mom and dad and
the frogs had to stay in the
pond. but every day gim
and betty go out to the pond
and see the frogs.

Now, obviously, all six stories leave a good deal to be desired
with respect to spelling, punctuation, paragraph, and sentence
construction. Each has potential, however, and in its own way each

also communicates. We would hope that whatever your child produced, you would compliment him and file the story to be used in future skills lessons as will be explained in Chapters Five through Eight.

ACTIVITY #2
Comic Strips

Sometimes a single picture is not enough to evoke anything more than a few descriptive sentences. While there is nothing wrong with writing of this sort, it may eventually become tiresome. Children usually enjoy *action* in their stories, whether reading or writing, but often have difficulty piecing together a coherent narrative.

One way to get around this problem is to present a *series* of pictures which themselves suggest a story. The child can then be asked to write his own story based on whatever the pictures suggest to him.

The most accessible source of these illustrations is undoubtedly the comic section of your local newspapers. (The Sunday edition is especially good since its comics are normally printed in color, as are comic books.) Selecting the frames will probably require a bit of editing on your part since consecutive ones are not always appropriate for writing purposes. If you save several days worth, however, you should be able to piece together pictures that can be incorporated into a very adequate story, especially if the child is familiar with the characters involved.

All that is really necessary to complete this activity, once the pictures are selected, is to cut out a few frames, mark out the written commentary, and attach them to a sheet of paper. Ask the child to write the story the pictures tell. To maximize the potential of this activity you can present several picture combinations and allow a choice. After some experience, the child can be given picture frames to put in any order he pleases (or given comic strips and magazines to search through to construct his own picture sequence).

Below are two sets of pictures we presented to several children who were simply asked to write the story they saw.

The least descriptive story we received consisted of four words:

Story #1

It was a rober

Many of our other stories were quite descriptive but devoid of punctuation, probably because the students were in the first half of second grade.

Story #2

Their is a rober and he is going to go in some ones house and take someting and he has a bat (note that the bag could be mistaken for a bat or club) in his haed and the dog woke up and he ran away and he did not take no toys or many ro tvs not a thing he did not gat in to gat someing he had a hat and glasses on the dog was littel

Story #3

THE ROBER

The rober is going to rob a house and Sunndly a dog Jummt from a boush and The Rober runs away, and The cops gets him and puts him in Jail and he hast to stay in thayer 50 days and that's The end of the rober

Story #4

the cruck did not see the dog and the dog was hideing from the cruck and when he came out he seen the dog and the dog startet to bard and the man ran

Undoubtedly, the first reaction of many parents to stories such as this is dismay at the absence of punctuation and capitalization, the many misspelled words, the presence of non-standard grammar, and the relatively poor organization of thoughts. We look at the situation somewhat differently, however.

To us the important point is that the cartoon frames were successful in eliciting written expression. For the most part, the children were able to tell us what the pictures meant to them through their available tools. True, they could not spell many of the words they needed; yet, in almost every case, they were able to put together a rendition that was quite easy to understand and made as much phonetic sense as the standard spellings (rober—robber; boush—bush; littel—little). In fact, the children's spelling bespeaks a strong phonics component in this particular school's reading program. It is also true that the grammatical aspects of the writings were not always standard English usages, but if it reflects the children's language (or the language in their homes), then that is fine. At this point, you are interested in fostering self-expression. Children will write as they talk or hear other people talk; there will be ample opportunities later on to teach the child to write in standard English when he so desires. In fact, we will teach you how to impose more structure upon your child's writing in future chapters. At this point, your primary goal is to get your child to *write*.

The next picture series was given to a slightly more advanced group of young writers. You should already be able to see an improvement in the mechanics of written expression, though the stories themselves are hardly more expressive or original. Your job as a writing teacher will be to find a way to gradually impose some mechanical restrictions upon your child's writing without dampening creativity and spontaneity.

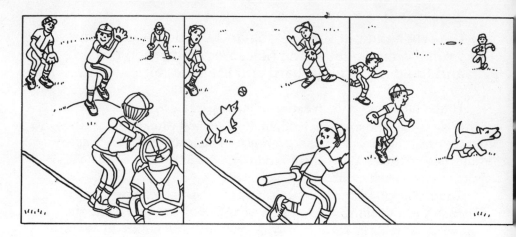

Story #1

One day five boys were playing baseball. One of the boys pitched the ball and another boy hit it. Then a dog came and tried to catch it. They boy that hit the ball fan to first base. The dog cart the ball. The boys ran after the dog because the dog had there baseball. The End

This first story is quite well-written story for a second grader. The sentences are well-defined and the spelling is not bad.

Story #2

The boys are playing baseball in the park. One boy hit the ball he was running to first base. The dog came in the park and got the ball. The dog went home. He froped the ball and the boys got it. And went back to the park. And started to play ball. The boy hit the ball out of the part and got a homerun. And it started all over again. With the dog and the boys.
                    The End

This too is well-written and the writer has added some creativity to it as well. If some of the periods are read as pauses, it flows well.

ACTIVITY #3
Supplying the Ending of a Story

Since you routinely read to your child anyway, it makes sense to use this experience occasionally to help foster writing skills. Select a story in which a good deal of action occurs at the end. (Detective or mystery stories are good candidates.) Pause just before the story's culmination and ask the child if he would like to write the ending to this particular story. If he seems to have trouble supplying one, you may wish to discuss two or three different possibilities first. You may wish to record the story on tape to allow it to be played back as many times as the child needs. (If he's too involved in the plot to brook such an interruption, don't force it; simply try again later with another story.)

Once the child's ending is constructed, read it orally, followed by the story's actual conclusion. Differences and similarities between the two can stimulate an excellent discussion. A variation of this activity is for the child to write the story and require you to supply the ending. (This will be especially fun for the child if you fail to guess the "correct" ending.)

ACTIVITY #4
Special Occasions

Holidays, approaching visits, and birthdays are all capable of stimulating the writer. Below are some examples of stories written by eight and nine year old children before the advent of Halloween.

Story #1

HALLOWEEN
Halloween is fun you ken
go trick r treating to go
frum house to house we get
a lot of cande in bags   The
ladeys give us cande. We
make eyes on the pupkin and
we weyr kostoms   I make tem
give me cande every Halloween
and we have a contest we haft
in the wober.

Story #2

HALLOWEEN
On Halloween ghost and witchs and golin
come out   People and children go out and
do shopping for candy.

You should cheak your candy because it
might hav bad tings end it.

Last day me and Jeannie and Judy and
Tamy saw a bat.   and I and my
cousin Jeannie was sraced to.

Note that both of these stories are quite interesting accounts of what Halloween means to the writer. The first is entirely personal. Though spelling expertise is limited and most sentences end without periods, the writer is easily understood. The second story begins with generalizations and becomes personal. The writer, who is on a higher reading level, also spells much better. She too could use some help in sentence construction, although we suspect that if she had read her story aloud, the "last day" might have been changed. Both children could benefit from work in Chapter Six at another time.

ACTIVITY #5
If I were a _____

This is an old stand-by of classroom teachers and it can work successfully for you as well. Children will imagine themselves as *anything* they like: an animal, a grownup with a special job, a plant, anything at all. If the child has trouble coming up with a topic, you can either suggest one or let him leaf through his picture books until something presents itself.

Here are some examples we have collected:

Story #1
IF I WAS A PETHER
I will clime on mountins in I will have a littel boy in a gail pether in I wad techa my boy in gail to clime trees in mountalns In techa them how to fite in my babys are 7 yira old

This is an example of a beginning second grade child's work who cannot yet spell or punctuate, definitely needs help constructing sentences, yet still expresses himself quite well. Our edited translation of his charming little story is as follows:

IF I WERE A PANTHER
I will climb on mountains and I will have a little boy and a little girl panther and I would teach my boy and girl to climb trees in mountains and teach them how to fight when they are seven years old.

In the next story we have an ambitious child with an active imagination. Note the dynamic name he has given his racing car: "The Fire Breathing Dragon."

Story #2

IF I WAS A CAR RACER

If I was a car racer I would go for
The championechip
I would win avery Time
I Rac and more I win the most
money I get   If I had to fac in the mud
spin mud on There car and make Them
loose and I would Be The winner of
all time my car would be The Best of
all Time   my cars name is the fire
breeva dragon

Other examples of topics chosen by children under our observation were:

If I was a Wich
If I were a Bird
If I Had Wings
If I Were Two Inches Tall
If I Were a Rich Queen
If I Were a Rabbit
If I Were a kitten
If I Were a Princess
If I were Dracula
If I was a deer

There is literally no limit to the possibilities. Help liberate your child's imagination and the result will be more creative writing.

ACTIVITY #6
Biographies

In school, children are often given assignments to write a paper about a famous leader, scientist, or other historical figure. Assignments such as this will be far less threatening if you give the child some early practice in writing about someone or something with which he is very familiar. Examples of topics are:

1. parents
2. siblings
3. a favorite pet
4. a wild animal
5. a relative
6. a fictional character such as Peter Pan, Cinderella, Robin Hood, or Peter Rabbit
7. a well-known historical character such as George Washington or Daniel Boone.

Before the child actually begins writing, offer some suggestions. When writing about a younger brother or sister, for example, suggest that the biography tell the child's age, name, and something which will distinguish him from other children of the same age. An excellent example of this type of writing (corrected for grammar and spelling) follows:

FREDDIE   *(edited)*

My brother's name is Fred, but we call him Freddie. He is two years old with brown hair, blue eyes and a little fat.

He likes to play with me and talk to me. Sometimes his words sound funny.

I like to play with him but not all the time. Sometimes he cries to go with me to school. That makes me laugh. I think how funny Freddie would look sitting in a big desk reading and doing math. Mother doesn't laugh about this, she just says, "Come on Freddie. You and I must stay at home."

Autobiography can also be quite useful in generating writing ideas. It can include basic facts about the child such as his age, sex, address, hobbies, and best friends, or it can focus on one specific incident such as the time he found a kitten, went to the hair stylist, rode a pony, and so forth. A good way to stimulate the first attempt is to read a short one aloud, perhaps your own. As with all these activities, you may have the child dictate the composition to you (or into a tape recorder) if the mechanics of printing appear to stifle creative output.

ACTIVITY #7
Letter Writing

Letters are one practical application of writing which the child sees constantly. Letter writing furthermore has a built-in advantage over practically every other type of writing; it is self-perpetuating. Nothing is more reinforcing to a child than receiving his own mail, so tell a grandparent or friend what you are trying to do. The incoming mail may be enough to keep the child writing letters. Be sure, however, that the people addressed are willing to answer promptly via letter and not telephone, since it is written communication which you are trying to foster.

Like other forms of written expression, letter writing does not spring forth in full bloom without some preparation. Initial efforts can be very elementary. Suppose, for example, a coat is received from a grandparent at Christmas. You could have a picture taken of the child in the coat and have the child write a sentence about it.

> Dear Grandmother,
> Here I am in my beautiful new coat.
> Thank you,
> Nancy

With experience letters become longer, although it is doubtful they will ever be better received. A simple format[1] that you can teach for these letters follows:

---

1. No single letter format will please everyone. There are many variations which are equally acceptable. Whichever you choose, however, strive to be consistent. Don't change the rules in midstream.

6633 Center Street
Friendly, New York 19777
(a) March 9, 1979

(b)

(c) Dear Jane,

   (d)

   (e) (Message)
I got the pictures your father took at your birthday
party. I sure wish I could have been there. Maybe . . .

        (f)

        (g) Your friend,

        (h) Mary

(a) Child's address
1. Capitals for the name of the street, the word street (or avenue, lane, circle, and so forth), the name of the city, state, and month.
2. The name of the city and state are separated by a comma. The date and year are also separated.
3. Abbreviations may be used in less formal writing.
(b) Space left between child's address and the greeting.
(c) The greeting is followed by a comma. If abbreviations are used, such as "Dear Mrs. Brown," the abbreviated title is capitalized and ends with a period.
(d) Space
(e) The message should be written in clear, well-worded form. Letters are one form of writing which should be edited by the child with your help.
(f) Space
(g) The closing is begun to the right of the center line. A capital is used in only the first word; a comma follows the last word. Show the child the different options available (for example, "Yours truly," "Love," "Sincerely," "Fondly," and so forth.
(h) The child's name

Other special occasions abound which can supply letter writing practice. A birthday party, for example, can be used to teach the child to write invitations such as:

421 Belgrade Avenue
Belgrade, Maryland 21214
March 6, 1980

Dear Bob,

Please come to my house for my birthday party on Saturday, February 3, at three o'clock.

Johnny Brown

Once written, the child can copy this form for all his invitations, although if they are to be mailed, you might do well to help address them.

Many other excuses exist for letter writing. Parents normally think only in terms of personal letters, but there is really no reason why children can't write business ones as well. The child could request free information from a travel agency or Chamber of Commerce regarding an upcoming family trip, for example, or he could order something advertised in one of his magazines using part of his allowance. The possibilities are endless and it is a shame not to explore at least some of them.

ACTIVITY #8
Definitions

Composing definitions can help the child bring more focus to writing. It is not as easy as it appears at first glance, especially for words that are very familiar. You might begin a lesson by picking a word and asking what it is.

For example, "What is a book?"

More than likely, the child will reply, "Something to read."

This, of course, is not a very specific definition, although from the child's perspective it does tell exactly what a book is. Asking further questions is a good way to get the child thinking: "Then is a newspaper or a letter a book? They are something to read."

The child knows that newspapers and letters are not books, but may be at a loss to explain why not. In this particular case, the dictionary isn't much help either, telling us that a book is printed sheets of paper fastened together at one side between covers and distinguished from magazines with respect to length and form.

This particular definition is a little unwieldy for a young writer, but a quite adequate attempt might have been:

A book is a bunch of typed pages stuck together between two covers. It is longer than a magazine and doesn't have advertisements.

You will find that in most cases children need more than one sentence to define even the simplest words. At first, you should allow your child to be as expansive as he wishes since this fits into the overall objectives of the present chapter. Later, you may wish to begin encouraging more economy of language, for which purpose Dr. Harvey S. Wiener[2] provides an excellent system for helping children frame useful, succinct definitions of common words.

Dr. Wiener suggests defining a word in general, then specific, terms. The following diagram illustrates how the system can be used:

word	"is"	general group	specific group
A store	is	a building or room	where things can be bought.
A school	is	a building	where children go to learn.
A bird	is	an animal	that has wings and can fly.
A potato	is	a vegetable	with a brown skin that grows under the ground and is good to eat.

If your child enjoys this activity, he may wish to construct his own "dictionary," possibly defining one word per letter. Allow as much practice with the activity as time and interest allow. Not only will its use help expand the child's vocabulary and teach the use of the dictionary, it will also encourage him to use more precise language in his other writing.

Don't worry if the definitions are not perfect. The one above for "a bird" does not exclude the bat as a possible category member

---

2. Harry S. Wiener. *Any Child Can Write*. McGraw-Hill Book Company. New York: 1978.

(though adding "that lays eggs" accomplishes this), while unjustly excluding the ostrich. Don't be overly picky at this point. Simply try to encourage the maximum amount of precision allowed by your child's limited experience.

ACTIVITY #9
Riddles

Rare indeed is the child who does not enjoy trying to solve simple riddles. The Sunday comics usually contain a section devoted to them, as do many comic books and children's television shows.

As much fun and as beneficial as solving riddles are, writing them is often even more popular. You may begin this activity by writing a sample for the child to solve, then encouraging him to try his hand.

Explain that a riddle is a type of guessing game with clues. It may begin with a general statement followed by sentences that narrow the field. The less detail supplied, the more difficult the riddle. Here are a few which a child might construct:

> I am very small. I have tiny ears and a long tail. I hate cats. What am I? (mouse)
>
> I look big to a mouse and small to an elephant. I go to school every day. I am eight years old. Who am I? (the child)
>
> I am thinking of something you can use often. It has a head and a foot but no neck or legs. I enjoy it most when it is clean and soft. What is it? (a bed)

You and your child can get hours of entertainment from this activity while valuable sentence and paragraph skills are being acquired. Don't hesitate to save the best efforts to try out on other family members. Your child will howl with delight if he is able to "stump" an adult with one of his riddles and probably will want to go right back to the drawing board to try again.

ACTIVITY #10
The Scrapbook

The activity we are going to discuss now is appropriate for both beginning and advanced writers. It is especially useful as a preparatory activity for reports or the type of writing assignments that children most often get in school, although it can be used remedially as well.

Let us suppose that you do have a child who, because of repeated failure in school, has lost all desire to learn to write. When an assignment is made, he hurriedly puts down a few sentences and hopes for the best, which in his case is that the teacher won't collect the papers or make him read his composition to the class. The next assignment will be a little more difficult than the one before (from which he learned nothing) and so things continue to get worse.

If you have a child in this predicament, you are going to have to break this chain of failure somehow. Chances are he will consider many of the activities previously discussed in this and the preceding chapter too childish, yet his skills don't warrant anything much more advanced.

One way around this dilemma is to suggest that he make a scrapbook on any subject he pleases. If he is interested in cars, trucks, airplanes, astronomy, sharks, birds, trees, sports, or anything else under the sun, fine. The important point is to begin with something in which *he* is interested, not an externally imposed topic which will make the activity burdensome.

After a scrapbook is secured, and this may either be a cheap commercial version or one the two of you make with a looseleaf notebook and construction paper, your first task is to begin gathering information. First, get all the materials you have at home from magazines, newspapers, and books. Next, go to the library with the child and take out what you need, making a note of remaining materials which may be helpful.

When you return home, have the child construct a title page containing his name, topic, and beginning date. Make sure that all needed materials are easily accessible, perhaps placed in a shoe box and kept with the scrapbook for convenience. (At one time or another, the following will probably be needed: scissors, crayons, pens/pencils, paste, tape, and lined paper.)

There are absolutely no rules as to how you proceed from this point. The child may wish to sort through all the pictures available to him, cutting out those from expendable sources, tracing the others, and pasting or taping them all in his book. He may then wish to title each and perhaps write a sentence or two about some of them.

Let's suppose your child chooses to do his first scrapbook on birds. After mounting all available pictures (without putting them in any particular order), he should begin reading some of the written materials he has gathered or, if they are too advanced, have you read them to him.

Encourage him to either make notes or indicate facts which he would like for you to jot down for him. Teach him to organize his thoughts by dividing the book into sections such as winter-summer birds, big-little birds, American-South American-African birds, and so forth, then subdividing each of these sections (for example, eating, making nests, and eggs). Once some plan has been generated, the pictures can be redistributed into the proper sections and the child encouraged to write sentences with facts concerning each picture (to supplement the titles, labels, and sentences he has already written), as well as introductory paragraphs for each section.

As always, allow him to dictate to you if his own printing is not sufficiently advanced, although this task can be made easier by your supplying a list of words which you know he will need. For example, when writing about nests, you could provide the following word list:

build, sticks, nest, bill, Father, Mother, construct, materials, mud, limb, tree, high, eggs.

As is probably evident, there is no natural end to this activity. Continue it until your child's interest begins to wane, then pick another topic and start another scrapbook. If at some time in the future his interest is rekindled in birds, or if something interesting is read concerning them, the old scrapbook can be taken out, reread, and additions made. Not only can they serve as a valuable writing activity and record of writing progress, they also serve as precursors of the more formal reports which will be discussed next.

ACTIVITY #11
Reports

Once the child starts school his formal writing assignments will invariably take the form of reports on one topic or another. While providing writing practice, the average school-based assignment still leaves a great deal to be desired.

In the first place, classroom teachers are often too busy to spend the time on an individual paper required to make it a real learning experience for the child. Added to this is the simple fact that children are seldom given sufficient instruction in *how* to write reports, a situation which often results in their simply copying paragraphs from an encyclopedia and, incredibly enough, receiving a passing grade for doing so!

You can circumvent this problem by teaching your child yourself to write reports. In some ways report writing is easier to teach than other types of writing because, by definition, less creativity is required on the child's part and his work is, therefore, more subject to correction.

When a child is asked to write a report on a topic, he is being asked to discover and write details which are not presently known to him. This implies research, analysis, and synthesis skills not normally found in a young child's repertoire of skills. There is, however, no reason why even very young children cannot engage in this form of writing with enough guidance. Certainly your time will be well spent; few skills are more important to your child's ultimate success in school.

Approach this activity both deliberately and cautiously. Communicate to the child that this is a different type of writing whose purpose is to *teach* whoever is to read the report something about the topic in question. For that reason, it must be written very carefully and correctly.

Below are a few steps which you should find useful in generating early attempts at report writing:

1. *Define the topic carefully.* Inexperienced writers usually have a great deal of difficulty writing reports for the sole reason that they begin with a broad, unfocused topic. The child who tries to write a report on Canada, for example, is going to run into trouble. Entire libraries are written on Canada and Canadian related topics. How is a child going to be able to put together a coherent report on so broad a topic in two or three paragraphs?

"The History of Canada" or "Canadian Geography" isn't much better. Teach the child to narrow his focus, then narrow it again. This will not only improve the report, it will make the task seem more finite and less threatening, preventing that helpless feeling of not knowing where to begin or how to proceed. It will, in other words, allow him to "get started," which is always half of the battle in writing.

One way to narrow the scope of the assignment would be to find out one thing the child would like to know about Canada and make that the research topic. How big it is, for example; who the first explorers were; what type of animals are found there; or even where the country is located, are all much more manageable bites for a beginner. This skill of coming up with a focused, sufficiently narrowed, topic will serve the child well throughout his academic career.

You may teach your child to narrow his topic of interest in two ways. In the first place, you can offer him potential topics based on subjects which you know are of interest. You may also enlist his aid in coming up with topics that interest him personally. Solicit as many as he can think of, narrowing each to a specific question before writing it down. Keep a list of topics for future use, adding to it each time your child asks you a question about something or as you observe his interests via television documentaries, pictures in books or magazines, and the like.

2. *Choose suitable references.* Unlike the other types of writing discussed so far (with the exception of the scrapbook), reports require the gathering of information outside the child's repertoire of experiences. This necessitates locating suitable sources for that information, a skill which very few children are able to pick up on their own.

In the beginning, you will probably be better off keeping the number of references to a minimum. Sometimes, of course, a topic will be suggested by a book or an article in one of the child's magazines, but in most cases his primary sources of information will be the dictionary and the encyclopedia.

In the original example concerning the size of Canada, many dictionaries will supply a surprising amount of information such as the number of square miles, the population, and the country's location. From this information alone a quite reasonable beginning report could result.

HOW BIG IS CANADA?
Canada is a big country. It has 3,852,000 square miles. It is bigger than the United States of America. The United States has more people.

Now, of course, primary grade youngsters are not going to be able to use dictionaries routinely without a great deal of help from you, but there is no reason why you shouldn't help the child as much as he needs in the beginning. You can suggest a reference, show the child how to locate facts in it, and read passages to him pertaining to the topic. You can even show him how to organize and write his report, gradually supplying less and less direct help as more experience is gained.

The best references, of course, are those which the child can learn to use and read himself. The Golden Book series puts out relatively inexpensive beginning encyclopedias. *My First Golden Encyclopedia* for preschool and the early grades followed by *The Golden Book Encyclopedia* for slightly older children are also possibilities. In addition, *Compton's Preencyclopedia* for beginners and *The New Book of Knowledge* or *Britannica Junior* are more suitable for slightly older children.

Some of these children's encyclopedias provide a wealth of information for report writing in language the child can both read and understand. If you decide to purchase a set, be sure that you get your money's worth by using them on a regular basis in planned writing activities.

3. *Taking notes.* No one, especially a child, should ever try to write a report from memory. Instead, supply index cards and have the child write the name of the reference at the top of the card with pertinent information underneath. *Do not permit the verbatim*

copying of sentences. If you do, the final report will probably wind up being a simple copy of the sources(s) used. This is a natural behavior for children and should be prevented before it ever begins manifesting itself.

SOURCE: Britannica Junior
TITLE OF REPORT: *Canada's Size*
population 22,300,000
                              most people live in eastern half
land . . . . 3,851,809 square miles
                              bigger than U.S.
                              many big lakes & rivers
location . . . . borders U.S. to the north
                              very cold a lot of year
                              bounded by three oceans
                              (Atlantic, Pacific, and Arctic)

If more than one source is employed, then separate index cards should be used. We suggest that you supply a file box for these cards and retain them after the final report is written, since they can often be used again for related reports or simply reviewed occasionally as a source of factual information.

4. *Organizing.* In the beginning it is too much to expect the child to construct a formal outline of his report prior to its writing. You can teach him to read over his index card(s), however, and decide what he will put in his paper and what he will leave out. (Children often feel that they must include all their notes and thus need to be reminded of the question(s) they are trying to answer by writing the report in the first place.)

When the child does become advanced enough to outline his notes, teach the following simple format in which the major headings are followed by phrases or complete sentences:

CANADA'S SIZE

I. Population
    A. Canada has 22,300,000 people.
    B. Canada does not have as many people as the United States.
    C. Most of them live in the eastern part of the country.

II. Land and Location
   A. Canada has 3,851,809 square miles of land.
   B. It borders the United States to the north.
   C. It touches three oceans.

5. *Writing the report.* Once the notes have been organized in this fashion, the actual writing is relatively straightforward. The child could even combine the six sentences in the above outline into a two paragraph report, although with a little guidance he will be able to combine sentences into a smoother flowing passage, as well as add something of himself.

CANADA'S SIZE

Canada has 22,300,000 people. This is not as many as the United States has.

Canada has more land than our country. It has 3,851,809 square miles. It is not as crowded as the United States.

It touches three oceans. The Atlantic Ocean is in the east. The Pacific Ocean touches the west and the Arctic Ocean is to the north. The whole country is north of the United States.

I don't think there are many countries as big as Canada. I don't think there are many that have so many oceans either.

6. *Editing.* As we have stated, report writing is different than other forms of written expression. The emphasis should be upon clarity and correctness; thus there is absolutely no reason why each composition cannot be edited for spelling and grammatical errors before it is considered completed. This process generally encompasses the following five steps:

   a. *Oral proofreading,* where the child reads the composition to you. This will help him identify blatant misspellings, incomplete sentences, and grammatical errors on his own.
   b. Having the child identify *"possibly" misspelled words* which you will then help him look up.
   c. *Silent proofreading* using an index card from which a three or four inch window has been cut. This forces the child to proofread his compositions two or three words at a time as

       the card is slid along each line, thus enabling more errors to
       be detected.

d. *Parent and child proofreading* where the two of you go over
the composition one final time with you identifying errors
and asking the child if he can guess how a word should be
spelled or how a sentence could be constructed to make it
"sound better." You may, for example, point to a misspelled
word and say, "I wonder if this is spelled correctly?" If the
child doesn't know, you can take him through the sequence
of steps suggested in Chapter Six.

e. *Recopying* if necessary to insure legibility (and rereading to
eliminate copying errors).

If you approach this task in the proper spirit, making a lighthearted game of it rather than an incriminating event, your child
will come to consider editing an integral part of writing and
gradually learn both to correct his own mistakes and avoid making
many of them in the first place.

ACTIVITY #12
Poetry

No discussion of children's writing could possibly be complete
without mentioning poetry. Poetry is as natural to childhood as the
jingles and chants permeating play (such as "Ring Around the
Roses," "One Potato, Two Potato," and rhythmic rope skipping
chants).

While children love the sound of rhyming words, rhythm,
meter, and economy of expression are also integral parts of poetry.
The only way we know to teach a child to appreciate all these
characteristics is to read poetry to him regularly.

You do need some understanding and appreciation of poetry to
teach your child to compose it, however, so if you are not comfortable with modern poetry, you should probably concentrate on
reading poets whose rhythms *both* you and the child can appreciate. Favor "heavy" rhythms and well-defined verse. Authors
such as Longfellow and Moore make excellent reading for children

since they cannot fail to hear the "beat" in the lines. Two of our favorites begin with:

Listen, my children, and you shall hear
Of the midnight ride of Paul Revere.   *(Longfellow)*

Twas the night before Christmas and all through the
     house
Not a creature was stirring, not even a mouse.   *(Moore)*

Anthologies containing nineteenth and early-twentieth century poets, or volumes such as Robert Louis Stevenson's *A Child's Garden of Verses*, can go a long way toward teaching the child to love poetry. Make sure you read them to your child, for poems must be heard to be appreciated. Favorites can be read time and again.

The haiku.[3] Perhaps the simplest type of poetry for a child to write is the Japanese convention called haiku (hī kōo). This poetic form, usually about one of the seasons of the year, consists of three lines: the first and third possessing exactly five syllables, the middle line having seven. Often the haiku begins with a general statement and ends with a concrete, surprising image.

The syllabic constraints of the haiku give it just enough structure to help, rather than hinder the budding poet. It is true that he may have to substitute word after word to achieve the exact number of syllables needed (and may require help counting them), but this is what poetry is all about: finding the exact combination and ordering of words which best express the feeling, emotion, or thought the poet wants to convey.

Below is an example of the type of haiku a child might write with assistance. To help yours get started, first write one yourself, then write the first line of another for him to finish.

Snap, crackle, and pop.   (5 syllables)
Pitter patter in the Fall.   (7 syllables)
Squirrels on the roof.   (5 syllables)

---

3. We are indebted to Anna Cosman (*How to Read and Write Poetry*, New York: Franklin Watts, 1979) and Dr. Harvey S. Wiener (*Any Child Can Write*, New York: McGraw-Hill) for their discussions of the haiku in children's writing.

Dark November nights   (5 syllables)
_____ (7 syllables)
_____ (5 syllables)

Couplets. As much fun as haikus can be to write, they don't employ rhyme and many children do enjoy that aspect of poetry. One way to get the young poet started is to teach him to write two-line poems which both rhyme and contain exactly the same number of syllables. For example,

Bobby acted like a clown   (7 syllables)
Every time someone fell down.   (7 syllables)

To get the child started, recite a couplet in which only the last word is missing, as in

Look who's coming, Mister Cat!
Always eating; he's so _____.   (fat)

After guessing the last word in a few couplets you make up, help the child construct some as well. Until he is good at it, don't worry about the number of syllables.

As with the haiku, you can supply the first line to get the child started, making sure the last word is an easy one to rhyme. Later, when the child becomes more proficient, couplets can be combined into longer poems.

Incorporating a School Assignment into Your Program

If your child's teacher gives you the go-ahead to help out occasionally with homework, written assignments can provide good forums for lessons. Suppose, for example, the homework assignment is to write about a recent trip.

The child's first reaction may be panic. He can't think of anywhere he's been recently. At first you can't either. You didn't go anywhere last summer, so what on earth can he write about?

Suddenly, however, you remember that the two of you did go to the library last Saturday. That should qualify as a trip, although a modest one. You try the idea out on your child and he is enthusiastic. A problem remains, however, with the audience for the paper. Who would be interested in a family trip to a library?

Certainly you can simply have the paper titled something like "A Trip to the Library" and make the child's teacher the *de facto* audience. A more creative approach, however, might be to ask the child who he would like to tell about the trip.

Suppose he comes up with the idea of telling his grandmother about the excursion. You could then suggest that the narrative be incorporated into a letter addressed to her. The next step might involve discussing the trip with the child for awhile, remembering things he saw along the way, his purpose for going in the first place, what he did once he got there, and so forth.

If your child's teacher permits parents to help spell words not found in his spelling book, you could write down certain words which you suspect may be needed in the composition, such as: library, librarian, shelf, building, card catalog, fiction, juvenile, Saturday, visit, interesting, quiet, borrows, and signature.

The child then writes the letter/composition, referring to the word list when necessary. Suppose something like this results:

> October 12, 1980
> 326 Weiner Avenue
> Harrington, Delaware 19951

Dear Grandmother,

Mother and I had a good trip Saturday. We went to the library. We had bin their before. We stad a long time. We looked at lots of books. The librarian showd us around.

I got a book to read. It was about boats. Mother says that as soon as I read it we will go on another visit to the library. I don't know what Ill get then.

> Love,
> Jim

Upon completion, the child reads you the composition. On his own he changes things that don't sound or look quite right, and you ask if there are any words he would like to look up. The misspelled words (bin-been, their-there, stad-stayed, showd-showed, and Ill-

I'll) were left uncorrected but recorded (without the child's knowledge) by the parent for future home spelling lessons (see Chapter Six). (If the parent corrects misspelled words in a homework assignment, the teacher has no way of knowing what the child's needs are.) Since the child has actually written a letter to his grandmother, you suggest that he copy and mail it to her. The assignment will then result in a return letter from his grandmother and, hopefully, praise from his teacher.

All homework assignments won't have such happy endings, of course, but you can usually keep them from being aversive experiences while ensuring that they serve the useful purpose they were designed for *if* this is consonant with the teacher's philosophy. If he/she prefers you not involve yourself in your child's writing assignments, then by all means comply. There are more than enough activities in this book for you to be able to teach your child to write on your own.

To summarize, the steps in helping with a writing assignment are:

Choosing a topic
Choosing a format
Discussing the ideas and writing vocabulary words
Writing
· Rereading and editing

More Ways to Write

No one could ever list all the possibilities for stimulating written expression in children. Childhood is a time of almost unlimited imagination which needs only the smallest spark for ignition.

The following list is a small sampling of additional ideas which can be used to encourage writing. Many of them are gamelike, but just as useful as some of the more structured activities discussed previously.

1. **"Why Things Are the Way They Are."** If you haven't read Rudyard Kipling's *Just So Stories* to your child, prepare yourselves for a real treat. Then encourage the child to write his own fanciful explanation of "evolution," such as "Why Turtles Carry Their Houses" or "Why Pigs Have Curly Tails."

2. **News Reporter.** Have the child write a news account of some actual or fanciful event for his own newspaper. Topics can range from actual or imagined world events to more mundane occur-

rences in the child's life elevated to exclusive status. He can even make a couple of copies and "deliver" them to family members.

3. **Create a Super Hero.** As all parents who allow their children to watch television or purchase comic books know, there is a bewildering abundance of characters with superhuman powers. There's always room for one more, however, so let the child invent one and describe his/her special powers. Later, episodes involving the character can also be written, thus providing an ongoing writing forum.

4. **Describe the Big Play in a Televised Ball Game.** If the child's father watches sporting events on television, an excellent opportunity for sharpening precise descriptions of actions is afforded. Have the child write about one event in the game in as much detail as possible to read aloud to fans.

5. **Rules for a Game.** Have the child describe in writing how a common game (checkers, for example) is played for a make-believe friend who is not familiar with it. In most cases the results will be completely bewildering, but the process itself affords excellent practice in using precise language as well as organizing one's thoughts. An interesting twist to this exercise involves your trying to play the game using only the child's written account. This will result in a great deal of fun and provide a non-threatening way of showing the child how he could have improved his description. Below is a description a child wrote for us about how to play baseball. Other possibilities include how to dance, throw a frisbee, or ride a bicycle. Humor can be added by describing mundane occurrences, such as how to eat, sit down, or brush your teeth. Thoroughness and logical organization of thoughts come only after years of practice.

HOW TO PLAY BASEBALL

First in baseball you have to have a umpire. then a picher. and first base men. a second basemen. and third base men. and also Bases. first base second Base and third base. and home. then the umpire says play Ball! and the pitcher piches the Ball. and then the man thats hitting hits the ball then runs to first base. then somebody els hits when he hits the Ball then the man that hit the ball first—runs to second base. then when some body els hits one over the fence—all the gys have a home run. and there realy happy. the end.

6. **Directions.** Most children are quite poor at both giving and following directions. Like the previous two suggestions, communicating directions on paper requires precise descriptive writing. Don't be surprised if you get results like the following edited example which occurred when a child wrote how to get from his school to the post office six blocks away:

> Go out the door and turn right. Walk two blocks and turn right and walk a while. You might get tired before you see it.

Asking questions often helps to achieve more explicit instructions. Also, as in the previous activity, one effective way to point out the need for greater clarity is for the two of you to start off to actually find the location by relying solely on the child's written directions.

7. **Pretending to be a Favorite Character.** All children fantasize about being a favorite character (for example, Superman, Captain Kirk, or Wonder Woman) in their play. Why not let them do the same thing in their writing, constructing a short episode with themselves as the character in question?

8. **Happiness is _____.** You're probably familiar with the cartoons captioned "Love is . . ." followed by a little homily of some sort. Charles Schultz does the same thing with his *Peanuts* characters occasionally, so children are usually familiar with the convention. To use it in writing simply let the child complete the sentence and add a few more lines to more fully describe the situation, be it real or fanciful. Other roots are:

> Being afraid is _____.
> Being lucky is _____.
> Being mean, nice, brave, and so forth, is _____.

9. **How _____ was he?** Almost all children enjoy hearing tall tales like those involving Paul Bunyon and his blue ox. Given half a chance they'll also enjoy writing them:

> (Child) You should have seen the tall basketball player I saw on T.V. yesterday.
> (Parent) How tall was he?

(The child writes)   He was so tall that he had to bend down to put the ball through the basket. Once he jumped so high that he got pieces of cloud in his mustache. I've heard that he's so tall that birds build nests in his hair.

Make sure that you reinforce tall tales by laughing and marveling at their improbability.

10. **Diaries.** Diaries are a different literary form from the autobiographical sketches previously discussed. They involve recording day-to-day occurrences and private thoughts the child would like to remember. The chief difference between diaries and other types of writing is in the audience for whom they are intended. You should respect the private nature of the diary and remember that it serves two important purposes: it assures that the child will engage in some writing on a very regular basis *and* it provides for an emotional outlet far more healthy than most available to us. Your only role in diary writing is to supply the child with an appropriate one (the type with a lock and key are very popular with children) and encourage its being kept up-to-date.

11. **Book Reports.** There are two ways of looking at requiring the child to write a book report each time he finishes reading something. One is that the assignment provides an excellent stimulus for encouraging the child to write. On the other side of the coin, however, is the possibility that the task can become so unpopular that it takes much of the joy out of reading.

A compromise between these two extremes might be to require routinely that your child simply write down the title and author of each book he reads (or that is read to him) along with perhaps one or two sentences describing what the book was generally about. These brief synopses can be written on index cards and made into a personal card catalog which can serve as a permanent record of his reading. Only very special books, then, would rate a full-fledged report telling what the book was about in more detail and the child's reaction to it. (Be sure to encourage honest appraisals; it is perfectly natural for some books not to be enjoyed.)

Another option popular with many children is to construct a *jacket* for a newly read book complete with title, author, illustration, and blurbs about the book's content either on the inside flaps or back cover. If the book already has a cover (most children's books do not), you may take it off before the child reads it and later compare his version with the publisher's.

12. **Making a list of writing ideas.** We have by no means exhausted the possibilities for stimulating writing experiences. Undoubtedly, both you and your child can come up with enough new ideas to keep you in topics for years, so you may find it profitable to keep your own file. Let the child come up with most of the ideas and give him a veto power over those you generate. Then, when the day comes that the two of you can't think of a suitable topic, simply take out the idea file and sift through it until something strikes the fancy.

With a little effort and a lot of interest on your part, this and the other activities presented in this chapter should keep your child writing for years. Enjoy.

5

Writing Sentences

A five-year-old child already has a good intuitive understanding of what a sentence is. Even though he hears and talks in sentences, however, it is not until he begins to read and understand punctuation that the concepts distinguishing words from sentences start to crystallize. Even then he is by no means ready to write and punctuate grammatically correct sentences on his own.

Sentence construction is not a skill that can be picked up overnight. Even when simple sentences can be written in isolation it may take a good deal of practice before they are seen used correctly in compositions. This is quite natural and we suggest that you continue to encourage your child to express himself via the activities in Chapter Four while working in isolation on the skills in this chapter. In other words, if your child writes on one particular day, you might teach the sentence construction lessons on another. (The same is true for the other skills presented in Chapters Six through Nine, for although the study of sentences constitutes the first skill chapter, we do not expect you to complete it before beginning the lessons in the other chapters.)

In this chapter a series of increasingly complex exercises are used to heighten awareness of both what constitutes a sentence and how sentences are written. In each case you will guide the child by using his prodigious gift of knowing "what sounds right" to achieve success. This will only work, however, if the child hears complete sentences spoken in his home environment. You must, therefore, make sure that the grammar and vocabulary you use with your child is consonant with what you want him to learn. Examine your own speech patterns carefully and, if need be, make a special effort to use grammatically complete sentences whenever possible. (Reading to the child is one way to facilitate his acquiring this "sentence sense.")

How to Use This Chapter

Which of the activities contained in this chapter will be too easy or too hard for your child depends upon past language and writing experiences. It never hurts, however, to start with extremely easy activities to give the child a feeling of success. Some of the early ones can be played as games with children as early as the fourth year, although their real utility lies with beginning writers who tend to either break up sentences into brief phrases or to connect long strings of simple sentences with the word "and." Here are some actual examples of each problem using the burgler cartoon presented in Chapter Five.

Story #1

A man running with a bag in his hand. And a dog by the bush. Running from a house. Running in the grass. coming to a house. And he saw a dog. come out of the bushes. he ran away. Because the dog scared him.

Story #2

The cruck did not see the dog and the dog was hideing from the cruck and when he came out he seen the dog and the dog started to bard and the man ran.

If your child has progressed in his writing to the point of having one of the above problems, then he is ready to proceed with the activities in this chapter. Don't worry if the first few are too simple for his particular stage of development. Simply breeze through them as quickly as possible and go on to more appropriate ones.

ACTIVITY #1
Listening for Real Sentences

Even though most children would be at an utter loss to define a sentence, they can pick out strings of words that sound "right" from those which do not. The following is a game-like activity you can play frequently at your leisure by inventing strings of words.

To begin, read aloud each pair of word strings. Ask the child: *Which one sounds right* or *Which one sounds like something you might say?* After each correct answer, tell the child: *Yes. It sounds right because it is a sentence and tells us something.*

Exercise A
(If clarification is needed say "Which one is not silly?" or "Which one would you say?")

It's my doll.	room car nose
Where's your coat?	is was have
fast big too	What's your name?
dog the see	See the dog.
Throw the ball.	ball the throw
Tie your shoe.	shoe tie your
going is home John	John is going home.
He's a boy.	boy a he's

Exercise B
The child should be familiar with the term "sentence" from Exercise A. Now it is time to force him into making fine discriminations. Ask, *Which one is a sentence?* If the correct response is not known, simply repeat the two forms and ask which "sounds the way we talk?"

The dog is next to the pony.	dog next to pony
I want more milk.	more milk
the bird	The bird is in the tree.
Let's read a story.	let's read story
the girl here	The girl is here.
My name is Bobby.	my name Bobby
I have a new toy.	I have new toy

ACTIVITY #2
Correcting Sentences by Listening

Read each sentence to the child and ask him to correct it.

DIRECTIONS: *Now I'm going to read a sentence that has something wrong with it. I want you to say it the right way.*

Mary and Nancy are a girl.   (are girls)
Bobby and Danny are a   (are boys)
   boy.
Sue and Ann are a child.   (are children)
I are going home.   (am going)
He are at school   (is)
They go at the store.   (to)

You should make up additional exercises based upon your child's particular needs. Take note of his speech and writing patterns, emphasizing areas in which he has problems.

ACTIVITY #3
Completing Sentences by Listening

DIRECTIONS: *I'm going to read you some things that only need one word to make them into sentences. See if you can think of a word for each one. (Any word which completes the sentence correctly is acceptable.)*

The dog ＿＿＿＿＿＿.   (barks, runs, etc.)

The girl is ＿＿＿＿＿＿.   (here, pretty, etc.)

I have a new

＿＿＿＿＿＿.   (coat, toy, etc.)

I have _____ new toy.   (a)

I like to _____.   (play, eat, etc.)

I like my _____.   (mother, bicycle, etc.)

ACTIVITY #4
Completing Written Sentences with Pictures

From the previous exercises the child already has an understanding that a sentence embodies a thought. Now that sentences will be presented in visual form, it must be pointed out that they always begin with a capital letter and end with a period, question mark, or exclamation point (for the time being we'll deal only with periods). In this exercise the child completes sentences with pictures and objects.

Print the following sentence stem on a piece of heavy paper or cardboard, leaving a large blank followed by a period.

I see a _____.

Collect an assortment of small objects and pictures of objects and label them clearly. For example, you might have a cup, a pencil, a book, a toy car, and pictures you draw of a dog, a girl, a boy, and a tree. Read the sentence stem to the child and ask him to put an object or picture in the blank to make it a sentence. Each time he should read the new sentence aloud.

If suitable pictures depicting action can be found or drawn, the exercise can also be completed using missing verbs. Employing a sentence stem with the child's name is always enjoyable:

(Child's name)   likes to _____.

Pictures that could go in the blank might be labeled "eat," "run," "walk," "sing," "dance," "sleep," "sit," and "play."

This is a game for which you can make up numerous variations on your own. Animal names are always well liked. Given a stem, "Rabbits _____." the child could draw pictures which you would label "hop," "run," "eat," and "play."

ACTIVITY #5
Completing Written Sentences with Words

This activity continues the work with stems to make simple sentences. Now, however, words are used instead of pictures and the child copies the sentence on his own.

On a sheet of paper write the following words: book, boy, girl, hat, tree. If your child cannot read any one of them, draw an explanatory picture next to it, then print the following sentence with a large blank beneath the last word.

Here is a _____ book _____.

Help the child read the sentence. Then ask him to copy the stem "Here is a" four times changing the last word each time to one of those in the list. Be sure he remembers to begin with a capital letter and end with a period. Have the sentences read until you are reasonably sure that all the words are recognized.

Using the same list of words, work in a similar manner with the following stem:

This is a _____.

Once the exercise has been completed the child will have written nine different words: Here, is, this, a, book, boy, girl, hat, and tree. You can now demonstrate that these same words can be placed at different points in the sentence and express the same or nearly the same idea.

Here is a book. . . . . A book is here.
This is a book. . . . . This book is here.

Give some practice in reading and writing these sentences. Point out that "here" began with a capital in the first sentence, but does not in the second because it is no longer the first word. *Always* have the child correct a sentence that he writes without proper capitalization and punctuation. This can be done gently by saying *"Did you forget to do something to your sentence?"*

ACTIVITY #6
Unscrambling Sentences

Print each of the words in the following sentences on a separate
3″ × 5″ index card. (Also draw a large period on one card.) Give the
child enough cards for one sentence only in mixed-up order. Ask
him to unscramble the words to make a sentence. (Since the first
word will be capitalized, it will provide a hint.)

The here book is	The book is here.
at Look me	Look at me.
he Here is	Here he is.
children The to park the went	The children went to the park.
boys ride The bicycles on	The boys ride on bicycles.

Longer sentences can be invented as proficiency is gained.

ACTIVITY #7
Constructing Sentences with Word Cards

This activity differs from the last one in that the child makes up
his own sentences, given a selection of word cards from which to
choose. If you are using our reading program, your child undoubtedly has a sizable number of words which he can read written on
index cards. If not, copy some words from the picture dictionary
onto cards. Write each word in lower case letters on one side and
with the first letter capitalized on the other, so that it could be used
as the first word in a sentence. Make sure you also print up
additional cards containing verbs (especially *is* and *are*) as well as
commonly used words, such as *a, and,* and so forth. (You should
also make several "punctuation cards" containing periods and
question marks.)

After demonstrating the process a few times, give the child the
cards. Each time he puts together what he thinks is a sentence,

have him read it aloud to be sure it makes sense. If it doesn't, ask what additional words are needed. As always, make sure each sentence begins with a capital letter and ends with a period.

ACTIVITY #8
Writing Descriptive Sentences

Colors can be used to both encourage the writing of simple sentences and to elaborate upon those already formed. It may be helpful to create a special color card on which the color words are carefully printed in two columns with an appropriate crayon mark next to each.

—black   —purple

—blue   —red

—green   —white

—orange   —yellow

With the aid of a large number of sentence stems (which the child should help construct), practice can be afforded in the different uses of color words. Once the stems are ready, the child should write in the color words of his choice, referring to the color card for correct spellings:

My bicycle is _____.

My book is _____.

My room is _____.

My dress/shirt is _____.

OR

The car is ＿＿＿＿＿＿＿＿.

The tree is ＿＿＿＿＿＿＿＿.

OR

＿＿＿＿＿＿＿＿ is my favorite color.

Once sentences such as this can be completed without difficulty, you may leave the child to his own devices in constructing color sentences from "scratch."

Next, teach the child to use color words to improve upon some of the sentences written in previous activities,

This is a dog. . . . . This is a black dog.
A hat is here. . . . . A brown hat is here.

Certain words are especially helpful to beginning writers in making their sentences more descriptive, hence more informative. Since the child still may not spell very well, he will need to rely on you to supply many words. Sometimes, however, he may simply not be able to think of a descriptive word to use. Special reference cards containing groups of related adjectives can be useful.

We have already mentioned color words; other candidates for special reference cards include size words (big, little, fat, thin, tall, short, heavy, light), appearance (pretty, ugly, beautiful, blonde, brunette), temperament (bad, good, mean, kind, nice, sweet), and so forth. If these references are kept together and made readily available (perhaps in the beginning of the picture dictionary), their use will eventually improve the quality and description of writing. If adjectives are routinely added to the lists as they are encountered in the child's reading, his writing vocabulary will also be greatly expanded.

Another way to make sentences more descriptive is by providing detailed information. Use the example below to show how a sentence can be changed to "tell more", then work through the other sentences together. Hypothetical answers are in parentheses, but the possibilities are endless. *This exercise should show the parent the types of questions that can improve a child's composition by making it more descriptive.* The same questions may be used to expand the child's phrases into sentences. As always, make up additional examples.

EXAMPLE:
The boy went to the playground.
PARENT: *Which boy?*
(Jim went to the playground.)

OTHER SENTENCES:
The boys played a game.
PARENT: *Which boys?*
(Bob and Dick played a game.)
PARENT: *What game?*
(Bob and Dick played baseball.)

The girl went on a trip.
PARENT: Which girl?
(Nancy went on a trip.)
PARENT: *Where did she go?*
(Nancy went to visit her grandmother.)

We are going soon.
PARENT: *Who is going?*
(Sue and I are going soon.)
PARENT: *Where are you going?*
(Sue and I are going home soon.)
PARENT: *How soon?*
(Sue and I are going home in ten minutes.)

The turtle walked into the water.
PARENT: *What water?*
(The turtle walked into the pond.)
PARENT: *How did he walk?*
(The turtle crawled into the pond.)

ACTIVITY #9
Writing Dialogue

Children often enjoy writing sentences in which real or imaginary people and animals talk. One of the easiest ways of promoting this skill is by using sources with which all children are familiar: comic strips, cartoons, and comic books.

Start by cutting out a frame from one of your child's favorite cartoon characters. Next, scratch out the dialogue in the "bubble" over the talking character and ask the child to write what he thinks the hero might be saying in such a situation.

You can even draw a large bubble on a piece of primary writing paper with an arrow pointing to the attached cartoon. Encourage the child to write the dialogue in a complete sentence, after which you should enclose it with quotation marks, explaining that these little marks are how you let people know that someone is talking.

This single activity can give hours of enjoyable writing practice. The child can cut out his own comic frames and attach them to writing paper, or even draw his own. Allow him to regale other family members with fantasies or witticisms, writing anything he pleases as long as it is contained in complete sentences and is encased in quotation marks.

At some point you should, of course, teach the writing of dialogue in the context of a sentence so that dialogue can be used in a composition. To this end, you may construct exercises such as:

Mother said, "   ."
Daddy said, "   ."

or require the child to write the name of the speaking cartoon character in the original activity:

Spiderman said, "I've got you this time you crook."

OR

"Crime doesn't pay," said Superman.

Obviously, one of the ultimate goals of this type of exercise is to have the child incorporate dialogue into the types of writing described in Chapter Four. Chances are that with enough practice this transition will occur naturally.

ACTIVITY #10
Producing Sentences

This activity will help you discover whether or not the child can produce complete sentences without outside help. It can be repeated periodically to see how much progress is being made and how much more work on the previous activities is required.

Point to a word in the picture dictionary and ask the child for the name of the picture. Then, ask if he can write a sentence about the picture (or dictate one for you to write).

If he produces a sentence, compliment him, point out what he has done, and punctuate it appropriately. If he dictates a phrase, ask questions until he can expand the thought into a sentence. If trouble is still encountered, mention a grammatical sentence, asking if that was what he meant to say. Continue this process with different pictures for as many sessions as you judge progress is being made.

ACTIVITY #11
Asking Sentences

Your child has undoubtedly been introduced to the question mark through his reading. Reading questions and writing them are two entirely different skills, however, so at some point you will have to formally teach the writing of interrogative sentences.

Explain that when we need to find out something from someone, we ask them a question. Words beginning with "wh" help us ask, such as *who, what, when, where, why*, and *which*. Make up some examples to illustrate:

Who are you?
What is your name?
When are you going?
Where are you going?
Why are you going?
Which way are you going?
How are you going? (How contains "wh" but in a different
   order.)

Next, show the child that other asking sentences can be written
by simply changing the order of the words in a regular sentence:

The boy is here. . . . . Is the boy here?
I can run fast. . . . . Can I run fast?

You may construct exercises based upon this reordering principle. Be careful, however, because to the beginner it may prove
quite difficult. Below are some additional examples. Ask the child if
he can rearrange each sentence to make it into a question. (If this is
too difficult, supply word cards to allow physical manipulation of
the words, making sure each sentence is punctuated properly.)

He is a ball player.   (Is he a ball player?)
You are going.   (Are you going?)
Jan can dance.   (Can Jan dance?)
Nancy is a fast runner.   (Is Nancy a fast runner?)

To introduce the use of the "wh" words, present the child with a
group of simple sentences and have him write a question which
each could answer. For example,

Here is a rabbit could be the answer to *Where is a rabbit?*
This is a tree answers *What is a tree?*

Point out the fact that questions are answered with sentences.
After some practice, take the process one step further by one of you
writing a question and the other answering it. (Make your questions very simple.) For example,

QUESTION (Parent)	ANSWER (Child)
Where is my pencil?	Here is your pencil.
Who is my little girl?	I am your little girl.

or

QUESTION (Child)	ANSWER (Parent)
Where is Daddy?	Daddy is at work.
Where is Tommy?	Tommy is at school.

Variety may be added to this activity by using ideas from magazines or television shows to form the basis for questions. The sentences can gradually grow more detailed as in Activity #8. Also the more specific or involved a question is made, the more elaborate the answer must be. If the answer to a question is too complex for the child to write on his own, you may help draw it from him orally and print it yourself.

There are many variations to this activity, all of which will give practice in writing good sentences. You might, for example, have the child leave questions around the house for other family members to respond to in writing. It is also fun to hide a small present for the child who must guess its location or identity through writing questions or filling in stems such as

Is it in the _____?

or

Is it a _____?

Every simple sentence can be used to answer some question. Such questions are easily composed by starting with the word *do* or *does*. Work through the example together; then see if the child can write sentences for each of the questions, and questions for each of the sentences, below.

EXAMPLE:

Questions	*Sentences*
Do cats and dogs fight?	Yes. Cats and dogs fight.
Does mother like to read?	Yes.

Questions   *Sentences*
Does our family have
  a car?   Yes.
Do frogs swim in the
  pond?   Yes.

EXAMPLE:
Sentences   *Questions*
Mary goes to school.   Does Mary go to school?
John plays ball.
Ann and Sally walk to
  the playground.
The dogs love to jump
  and run.

ACTIVITY #12
Combining Sentences

The following exercises can be used to begin to provide the child with an alternative to short, choppy sentences. Don't expect smoother prose immediately, however. Be patient, and occasionally point out where these concepts can be applied in the child's written work.

and. The word *and* is often used to make one long sentence out of two shorter ones. Demonstrate with each example how the sentences below can be combined.

EXAMPLE:
Tom likes to play. Jim likes to play.
Tom and Jim like to play.

Mary eats fish. Jim eats fish.
Bob rides bikes. Bill rides bikes.
Sue likes candy. Ann likes candy.

EXAMPLE:
I saw a tree. I saw a bush.
I saw a tree and a bush.

I like apples. I like pears.
The boy is big. The boy is tall.
I have a new hat. I have new gloves.
Pam likes to run. Pam likes to play.
Father works. Father reads books.

The economy of using *and* can be dramatized by allowing the child to complete exercises such as this using word cards. Presented with two separate sentences made from cards the child can see how many words can be "saved" by using a single "and" card. Use many examples, some taken from the child's own writing when possible.

but. The word *but* is often used to combine two short sentences. Again, work through the example together and give the child the sentences below to connect.

EXAMPLE:
The little boy ran fast. The big boy ran faster.
The little boy ran fast but the big boy ran faster.

EXAMPLE:
Jane is older than Kate. She is not as tall as Kate.

I want to play in the snow. I have a cold.

Jim likes to play ball. Jill likes to play with her kitten.

Sandy likes juice. She doesn't like milk.

because. This word is very much a part of children's vocabularies. *Because* can be used to combine two sentences in which the second sentence answers the question "why."

EXAMPLE:

The man did not see the dog. The dog was hiding.
The man did not see the dog because the dog was hiding.

I didn't go to the movie. I didn't have enough money.

Dick laughed. He saw the clown.

The mouse ran away. The cat walked into the room.

I ate lunch. I was hungry.

if, when, before. Each of these words connects two thoughts in which one depends on the other. After looking at the example, copy the phrases in the two columns for the child to match. Note that when the *if* clause starts the sentence, it is followed by a comma.

EXAMPLE:

If it rains, we will not go.

If he comes early,	give her milk and cookies.
If she is hungry,	put him to bed.
If he looks sleepy,	give her a book.
If she wants to read,	ask him to wait for me.

I will run	when the music starts.
We will have dinner	when he hits the ball.
We will dance	when he sees the cat.
The dog barks	when it is cooked.

We must eat dinner	before having ice cream.
I will put away the ice	before nine o'clock.
He gets up	before it gets dark.
Let's go for a walk	before it melts.

Words that can be used to connect thoughts should be listed on an index card to be used as a resource when writing. Have the child read over the list a few times to insure familiarity with all the words. Here are some possible "connecters":

and	if	though
but	when	for
because	before	after

Improving Your Child's Writing

The activities in this chapter have given the child practice in recognizing and constructing sentences. Now it is time to apply the lessons to actual writing. (More sentence writing activities can be found in Chapter Nine.)

Compositions should always be read aloud by the child to the parent. Whenever a sentence fragment is used, ask the who, when, where, how questions that will enable the thought to be completed. If a sentence seems to run on forever, help the child separate out some simple sentences and use connecters where appropriate. When sentences are too general, ask questions to bring out more description. Always have the child read his work aloud as punctuated. If a period has been stuck in the middle of a sentence which necessitates a stop, for example, the child will better understand why it needs to be removed. By reading sentences aloud the writer can better judge himself whether they sound right. Your goal is for the child to be able to decide whether sentences are correct or not without your help. Once this can be done he will be well on his way to writing success.

6

Spelling

The beginning writer has one very large handicap. He will know the correct spelling of very few of the words he wishes to use, and therein lies a dilemma.

If given complete license to write words incorrectly over and over again, the child may come to memorize these incorrect spellings to such an extent that unlearning them may prove quite difficult. If, on the other hand, he is forced to look up (or ask about) the spelling of each and every word he wants to use, the joy of creative self-expression will almost certainly be spoiled.

What is obviously needed, therefore, is some kind of balance between the mechanical need for correctness and the creative need for freedom. We skirt this issue entirely for the child's first attempts at written expression by not requiring him to bother at all with such mundane concerns as handwriting, spelling, and punctuation. The child says what he wants to say and the parent writes it down. Only when he and his parent read the composition back together does he have contact with the written word, and even then he sees his creation correctly spelled, punctuated, and clearly printed.

Gradually, however, the child naturally begins to assume more responsibility for all phases of his writing. As he learns to read a few words and to write the letters of the alphabet, he will begin to copy some of the titles and simple stories he has dictated. With the growth of phonics skills he will invariably want to venture out on his own, using words he has not yet learned to spell.

It is at this point that the balance between complete freedom and an excess of imposed restrictions must be struck, a balance that will gradually but consistently shift over time. At first a great deal of freedom should be permitted, employing only informal techniques to improve the child's spelling. A few such strategies, all of which will be dealt with in more detail later, are:

1. **Parental help with spelling.** The parent is available should questions as to how to spell a word arise. Sometimes the answer is given outright, sometimes the child's help is enlisted to spell those parts of the word he can sound out.
2. **Special words are spelled in advance.** Before the child begins to write he is asked to anticipate any unknown words. Frequently he will ask for theme words such as Halloween, Christmas, birthday, and so on. These words are then written on a separate sheet of paper for easy referral.
3. **The child reads aloud.** Whenever the child has a finished product written he is probably anxious to share it with you. Have him read it aloud as you look over his shoulder. This way he may catch some of his own spelling errors and you will know what he meant to say. (Always show appreciation.)

Once these informal procedures are instituted, you must be disciplined enough to adhere to the program. Learning to spell is a complicated process which will take time and, in the beginning, a willingness to ignore the majority of the child's misspelled words to avoid spoiling the inherent joy in creative expression. Later on, when the child's reading ability permits, you will be able to use the actual spelling lessons described in this chapter along with the accompanying exercises involving: dictionary use, phonics, syllabication, endings, contractions, and special strategies for the problem speller.

How to Handle a Spelling Request

When your child is writing he may ask you how to spell a word. Never discourage such questions. It is natural that he turn to you for help. Your job now is to provide that help without breeding overdependence in the child. If you always tell him the spelling, he may forget the word as soon as it is written. Below are five questions you should ask yourself each time your child asks about the spelling of a word. They are based on the philosophy that *you should tell the child only what he can't figure out for himself.* Each step is explained fully in the discussion which follows.

1. Is the word in the child's dictionary?
2. Can the child supply the letters standing for the first sound? The last sound or any of the vowels? Can he spell any of the word's syllables?
3. Does he know a word belonging to the same spelling family? (For example, if he asks how to spell *band*, does he already know how to spell *hand* or *land?*)
4. Are any of the word parts familiar to him (for example, *-ing*, *-ed*, *-est*, *-tion*, *-ful*, *-fully*, etc.)?
5. Do none of the above strategies apply? Then simply spell the word for the child.

Dictionaries. Progress in spelling goes hand-in-hand with progress in the use of the dictionary. When the child asks you how to spell a word he should have already exhausted whatever dictionary resources may be within his grasp. The best way to encourage him to do this is not by chiding him for not trying to look a word up, however, but by taking the time to help him in his search. (Alphabetization and other skills necessary for dictionary use are discussed in Chapter Eight.)

In the beginning most commercial dictionaries are too difficult for the young writer to use as a serious spelling aid. This does not mean, however, that you should ever totally disregard this valuable source regardless of your child's age.

Alphabet books, for example, containing one word (with a picture) per letter are a type of primitive dictionary that can be used if the needed word happens to be included. One step more advanced is the picture dictionary whose construction we discussed in Chapter Four. The homemade version has the decided advantage over the commercial editions of being a flexible, living testament of the words the child actually uses in writing. (We don't wish to discourage you from purchasing one of these volumes; they can be quite useful. We just don't recommend that you *substitute* a commercial dictionary for the extremely valuable process of having your child construct his own.) Finally, if you are teaching your child to read (and we certainly hope you are), the Word Box discussed in *Teach Your Child to Read,* or the alphabetized glossary of words in the back of your child's school reader, can serve as an excellent source of correct spellings of common words.

The *Word Box* is a way of recording words that your child has learned to recognize. It is nothing more than a container for 3″ × 5″ index cards upon which words are written. It contains the child's entire repertoire of known words in alphabetical order. (Alphabetical dividers can be purchased to go along with the index cards.)

Since the child can read all the words in the Word Box, he can use it like a personal dictionary to look up any words he is not sure how to spell. If you have not compiled a Word Box, it may seem like an overwhelming task to start one now. Here is a way to begin such a device for the purposes of this chapter. Keep a list of all spelling errors made in your child's writing. Then make a list of these words spelled *correctly* and see which words he can read. Those and only those he recognizes go into the Word Box. Unknown words can go in a separate "New Words" envelope for reading and when learned can then be placed in the Word Box. If you follow this procedure consistently, over time your Word Box will be a nice spelling dictionary for your child.

We call these aids "starter dictionaries" because they can be successfully used well before the child is comfortable with a regular elementary dictionary. Each time he sits down to write he should have one or more of these sources beside him. If he then asks you to spell a word that you know is contained in one of them, you can say something like: "I wonder if that word is in your picture dictionary. Let's look and see." If he finishes a composition without requesting help and misspells a word contained in there, point it out as "possibly misspelled" and have it looked up and corrected. By patiently adhering to this strategy you will eventually get the child in the habit of looking up familiar words when in doubt.

It is possible to have too much of a good thing, however. When children first begin to print their own stories (as distinguished from dictating them), they know how to spell very few words. If they are required to look up practically every word they write, they won't tend to write many. Use your judgment, but don't require an inordinate amount of time to be spent looking up words. One or two per session is usually quite adequate in the beginning; more time can be spent following the story's writing (preferably at another session) if you deem necessary.

Phonics and Word Families. Suppose a word is not in one of the child's limited dictionaries. Do you have any option other than to simply supply the needed spelling?

In most cases you definitely do. Take the word "put." You would first call the child's existing phonics skills into play by repeating the word distinctly, then asking:

What letter could stand for the sound at the beginning of 'put'? If the child has learned beginning consonant sounds, he will probably answer "p." (If he hasn't, now would be a good time to start.) If he needs help in coming up with the letter, you might give him some other words that start the same way as cues (for example, *pay, party, pick,* and so forth).

Once the initial letter is guessed you could ask:

What letter could stand for the sound at the end? (Repeat the word.) If he does not know, you can cue him again or simply tell him. *Don't ask questions that the child doesn't yet have the knowledge to answer;* if that means soliciting only the first letter in "put," fine. Compliment him for giving the "p" and spell the rest.

By increasing his phonics skills the child will greatly increase his ability to spell because many words are spelled the way they sound. We say these words have *regular* spellings and in many cases can be grouped into word families. Let's say, for example, the child asks how to spell "fat" and he already knows "cat." Ask him what letter could stand for the first sound as above. Once "f" is given, tell him he knows a word that sounds like (or rhymes with) "fat" and is spelled the same way following the first letter. Write "cat" and "f" in the following manner for him to see:

$$\underline{c}\ \underline{a}\ \underline{t}$$
$$\underline{f}\ \_\ \_$$

Say "cat" and then the f (fff) sound and have the child repeat it. Next ask him if he can finish spelling "fat."

When helping your child with sounds in this way you may find it helpful to refer to the following chart of common vowel sounds. Both you and your child can then check it when necessary.

PHONICS VOWEL SOUND GUIDE

	A	E	I	O	U
long	ate	me	kite	no	use
short	at	met	it	not	up

Note that the long vowels sound like the letter names, while the short versions take on completely different sounds.

Also: When **y** follows a consonant at the end of a one syllable word, it sounds like the long **i** as in **my, by, try, fly,** and **cry.**
When **y** is found at the end of a word with more than one syllable, it sounds like the long **e** as in **daddy, very, pretty,** and **kindly.**

For a more complete discussion of phonics rules along with actual lessons for teaching them, see *Teach Your Child to Read.*

Word families once again are made up of words that are spelled the same except for the first letter (or couple of letters) and rhyme. Just as they are helpful in sounding out new words when reading, they are useful in spelling as well. If he needs to spell "place," for example, and already knows "face," the old word is brought up to help solve the new one. In this way, previous reading and spelling experiences can be used to directly foster spelling ability, just as they indirectly facilitate writing. The following Endings Table with examples of common families should help you identify suitable candidates for this process.

WORD ENDINGS TABLE

-ace/-ase	-ack	-ad	-ain	-air
place	black	sad	rain	fair
race	tack	bad	train	hair
face	back	glad	brain	chair
base		had		

-alk	-all	-am	-an	-and
walk	ball	Sam	man	band
talk	wall	ham	can	land
stalk	fall		fan	sand
	tall		ran	stand
	call			

-ank	-ar	-as	-ast	-at
sank	car	has	fast	cat
drank	far		last	rat
	star		mast	that
				mat

-ay	-aw	-eck	-ed	-ell
play	saw	deck	red	bell
day	jaw		bed	sell
stay	raw		sled	tell
tray			shed	well
way				
hay				

-en	-er	-est	-et	-ew
men	Father	nest	pet	new
hen	Mother	west	let	blew
then	hamburger	best	met	few
when	water		wet	chew
chicken			set	flew
children				

-ey	-id	-ide	-ig	-ight
they	did	wide	big	fight
	slid	slide	pig	bright
	hid	side	wig	light
		tide		might
		ride		sight
		hide		

-ild	-im	-in	-ink	-ird
child	Jim	tin	sink	bird
wild	swim	thin	drink	third
mild		chin		
		sin		
		win		
		fin		

-irl	-is	-it	-ite	-ly
girl	this	bit	bite	family
		sit	site	silly
		rabbit	kite	Billy
		wit		
		hit		
		lit		

-ode	-og	-om	-ome	-on
rode	dog	Tom	come	son
mode	log		some	ton
	hog			
	bog			
	fog			
	jog			

-one	-onk	-or	-ound	-ove
bone	honk	for	playground	love
			round	

-ow	-own	-oy	-uck	-ump
meow	town	toy	duck	jump
now	brown	boy	buck	
	clown	joy	luck	
			truck	
			stuck	

-un	-unk
fun	sunk
gun	drunk
run	
bun	

Spelling Lessons

Training the child to ask you how to spell words he does not know and then teaching him to supply some of the letters himself through phonics skills, while extremely valuable, will not completely do the trick. There is no way of getting around the fact that, to be competent spellers, children need formal lessons *after they begin reading at a second grade level.* Two to three sessions per week, thirty minutes or shorter in duration is ample. The remainder of this chapter is designed to show you how to conduct those lessons yourself.

How to select words for a spelling lesson. If your child is of school age and brings spelling words home from school, use them first. If not, or if you wish to supplement his instruction with age-appropriate words (and we recommend that you do), select words from his writings and the word list as explained below.

After the child has read his composition, show your appreciation for what has been expressed by complimenting him and hanging it up for others to read (or by filing it in a book with his other compositions as previously discussed). Selecting spelling words from his work is a job for you to perform in the writer's absence, for you must always try to disassociate the creative act of writing from any hint of failure on the child's part.

Record the date on which the work was written and *all* the misspelled words in a small notebook or pad. (Undoubtedly there will be many.) Next, refer to the lowest level words (Level I) on the spelling list at the end of this chapter. If any of the misspelled words are listed there, then they are your first candidates for a spelling lesson. Remember, however, that only one or two words need be chosen from any given story. There is no way that you are going to be able to teach all the words your child needs to know in only one or two lessons. To try would only be counterproductive.

Frequency of use is the next factor to look at. Are any of the words used more than once in the paper? Have any been recorded as errors on previous occasions? (A good way to ascertain this easily is to convert the contents of your notebook to 3″ × 5″ alphabetized index cards with the date(s) each word was misspelled recorded directly on the card. Words with more than one date then become prime candidates for a lesson.) Obviously, words that are missed most frequently *and* that fall lowest on the spelling list are the best choices, but if a difficult word is used over and over, it should be taught.

Finally, if your child is a reluctant writer and gives you little opportunity to discover a sizable number of words he cannot spell, simply start teaching the words at the beginning of the list and proceed from there in accordance with the teaching-learning strategy described below.

In summary, the four sources of words for spelling lessons are:

1. words given the child to learn at school,
2. incorrectly spelled words found in the child's writing which are found on the most elementary portions of the standardized spelling list presented at the end of this chapter,
3. words which are *frequently* misspelled (as shown by your ongoing records), and/or
4. words contained on the list presented later in this chapter.

How to teach your child to spell the words you select. We are going to recommend a method of teaching spelling that employs techniques going back many years to the work of spelling experts like Ernest and Thomas Horn. There is nothing new nor flashy about this teaching-learning strategy, but it has passed the test of time and it does work. To us that is the important thing.

Here are the basic steps:

1. **List Preparation**
   The parent compiles a list of two to five words for a spelling lesson using the criteria just discussed. To this, several words are added which the child *can* spell, such as from a previous lesson.
2. **Quiz**
   The first thing which is done with this list is to give the child a quiz. Since the quiz always contains known words, it will not be completely frustrating to him. Instructions can go something like this:
   I am going to read a few words for you to write down to find out which words you need to learn to spell. I will say each word, use it in a sentence, and then say it again. Write it down the best you can. If you don't know how to spell it, take

a guess from the way the word sounds. (Children with very little phonics training may simply write the first or first and last letters of the word.)

Give the quiz as described in the instructions. Make up sentences in which the spelling word is not the first word in the sentence. When reading a sentence, talk slowly and say the spelling word louder than the rest, but don't exaggerate any pronunciations.

3. **Quiz Correction**[1]

The Quiz Correction phase is an important procedure during which the child actually starts to learn the spelling words by detecting and correcting his own mistakes. Provide the child with a correct list of the quiz words to look at and have him correct his own paper while you spell each word aloud. He should write every word in need of correction again alongside the original attempt. Any wrong spellings the child does not catch can be pointed out by saying "Look again at this word."

Compliment the child on the words spelled correctly and ask him if they are already in his Word Box. If not, put them on cards and add them. The remainder of the quiz words should be printed on 3" × 5" cards and taken through each of the remaining steps in the teaching-learning strategy.

4. **Saying the Word**

Place the first word card in front of the child.

Look at the word while I say it.

Pronounce the word slowly and distinctly two times.

Now you say it.

5. **Oral Spelling**

Close your eyes, say the word, and try to see it in your mind.

After he does so:

Now open them and see if you were right. Look while I spell it for you. (Spell the word out loud).

Close your eyes, say the word, and try to spell it yourself.

After he does so:

O.K. Open them and see if you were right.

---

1. Adapted from Thomas D. Horn, "The Effect of the Corrected Test on Learning to Spell," *The Elementary School Journal*, January, 1947, pp. 277-285.

Keep repeating the procedure until the child can spell the word without looking. (For some children closing the eyes is not an aid to concentration. If this is true of your child, turning the card over, taking it out of the line of sight, or covering it with a shield can be substituted.)

6. **Written Spelling**

Once a word can be spelled in this way you should provide pencil and paper and instruct the child to:

Look at the word, then cover it up, and try to write it.

After this is done:

Uncover it and see if you were right.

The child repeats this writing procedure until he has done it three times in a row correctly.

All the new words on the spelling list are studied individually using the above procedure. Some children need a less intensive approach than this, thus the steps in which no difficulty is ever experienced can be omitted. (If your child doesn't really need you to pronounce and spell the word first, for example, just make sure that his pronunciation is correct. We suggest, however, that you follow the above procedure closely at first. It is better to give too much guidance than too little.)

Practice Techniques. Although most children learn their short spelling lists quite readily using the above teaching-learning strategy, some forgetting will surely occur without practice. We have found the following three techniques to be especially effective. Employ any which appear to work for you.

1. **Writing Drill**

The old standby writing drill is too often the only learning strategy employed in classrooms. Because no teaching is involved, the drill should only be used for practice *after* a lesson. It does have the advantage of being an independent activity which the child can complete on his own.

The writing drill is nothing more than having the child write each of his spelling words three or four times. It is extremely important, however, that the child check his spelling each time the word is copied. Too often words are written incorrectly several times in a row, resulting in memorization of the incorrect spelling. Children for whom writing is problematic (or beginning writers) should not use this technique.

2. **Picture Dictation**

   We first learned of this technique when reading a book written by W. Franklin Jones[2] over fifty years ago and have modified it slightly to better suit your needs. It is an activity that children enjoy doing on their own to practice spelling words. Only words which can be represented by pictures are included.

   The first step consists of the child going through magazines and cutting out pictures to match his word list. (Pictures may also be drawn by the child or another family member and, of course, if the word is already in his picture dictionary it can be used as well.) The pictures are mixed up, then selected one at a time. The child writes the word describing each on a separate piece of paper. When he is through he pulls out his spelling lists to check and correct his answers. The pictures are then filed away for future review.

3. **Practice in Context**

   You must never lose sight of the ultimate purpose of learning to spell correctly and that is to improve written communication.

   One way to facilitate this purpose is to have the child practice his spelling words in actual writing assignments. There are several ways of doing this, but two of the easiest are (a) to have him write a sentence employing each word in his list (you will worry about the spelling of the lesson word only), and (b) to dictate a short story to him using words he already knows but also including the spelling word several times.

The spelling words that have been taught and practiced should appear in future quizzes to check if they are still remembered. The real test of learning in spelling, however, is not a quiz, but a reduction of errors in the child's written work. It is there that you should look for improvement.

---

2. The *Jones Complete Course in Spelling.* Chicago: Hall & McCreary Company, 1924.

Syllables and Spelling

As useful as word families are, most words unfortunately do not qualify. In many instances, however, the child may still be familiar with the spelling of one part of a troublesome word.

Suppose, for example, that the child asks how to spell "hoping." Suppose further that he has already learned how to spell "going." It stands to reason, therefore, since one of our basic spelling tenets is to have the child supply all the letters of a word he can, that you would break up the word so that at least the "-ing" sound would be recognized.

To do this you might say something like the following:

Hoping. Hoping has two parts. Listen and see if you can hear them both: hope - ing. Hoping! Can you think of a word that you can spell that has a part like hope - ing?

If not, say: *Here is one word which also has two parts: going. Go - ing. Going. Can you spell going?*

If he has forgotten, help him. In any case write the word as follows:

go<u>ing</u>

Now say: *What part of going sounds like hoping?* Undoubtedly the child will say the "ing" sound.

That's right! Let's cover up 'go' so that we can see how to spell -ing.

Cover **go** with your finger.

How do you think we spell -ing in hoping? Allow the child to read the letters if he wishes.

Yes, we spell it i-n-g. Now I'll write the first part and you write the second.

You can then write **hop** and the child can add the **ing.**

The same procedure can be followed with other word parts such as "tion" (as in motion), "fully" (as in playfully), or any other word containing syllables that the child already knows how to spell. Before this can be expected to occur smoothly, however, the child's phonics program must be extended with an emphasis upon syllabication. In school this normally occurs around the third grade.

Take a spelling request for the word "vacation" as an example. Pronounce the word for the child, its parts syllable-by-syllable, then the word again:

vacation   **va-ca-tion**   **vacation**

Next, take each syllable one at a time and ask the child if he can name any letters standing for the sounds he hears. Write down whatever he comes up with, leaving space for missing letters. If the child has a good phonics knowledge, you may get something like **vacashun.**

Since this is an excellent phonetic rendition of the way the word actually sounds, acknowledge this to the child. Underline the portion that is spelled correctly and write the final part separately for him to look at. If he can read any words like "conversation" write them too and underline the **-tion.** Finally, write vacation and pronounce it together syllable-by-syllable and then as a whole before allowing the child to copy the word in his story:

<u>vaca</u>shun

tion   conversa**<u>tion</u>**

vaca**<u>tion</u>**

From this example it is probably obvious that phonics will help your child only to a limited degree. It will be extremely valuable in allowing him to spell by sound and be *understood,* but not as helpful in eliciting the *exact* spelling of a word. In words with more than one part, for example, the vowels in the unstressed syllables are often practically impossible to identify on the basis of sound alone.

Charles C. Fries,[3] the world famous linguist, points out how problematic this can be for the speller. The final vowel in words

---

3. Fries, C. C *Linguistics and Reading.* (New York: Holt, Rinehart, and Winston, Inc., 1963)

such as sofa, silken, victim, handsome, and lettuce all make the same sound (called the schwa sound) while each employs a different vowel. There are a multitude of such words which make life difficult for the beginning speller. He really can use his phonics skills only to spell those syllables in which the letters are in clear correspondence to the long and short vowel sounds normally taught in elementary phonics programs.

George Bernard Shaw probably sums the situation most succinctly with this little observation: "How do you pronounce *ghoti*, if the letters are pronounced as follows: **gh** as in rough, **o** as in women, and **ti** as in nation?" (The answer is **fish**.) An anonymous poet also questions the phonetic basis of our language:[4]

OUR QUEER LANGUAGE
When the English tongue we speak,
Why is "break" not rhymed with "freak"?
Will you tell me why it's true
We say "sew" but likewise "few";
And the maker of a verse
Cannot cap his "horse" with "worse"?
"Beard" sounds not the same as "heard";
"Cord" is different from "word";
Cow is "cow," but low is "low";
"Shoe" is never rhymed with "foe."
Think of "hose" and "dose" and "lose";
And think of "goose" and yet of "choose."
Think of "comb" and "tomb" and "bomb";
"Doll" and "roll" and "home" and "some."
And since "pay" is rhymed with "say,"
Why not "paid" with "said," I pray?
We have "blood" and "food" and "good";
"Mould" is not pronounced like "could."
Wherefore "done" but "gone" and "lone"?
Is there any reason known?
       And, in short, it seems to me,
       Sounds and letters disagree.

---

4. The authors acknowledge Tiedt, I. M. and Tiedt, S. W. *Contemporary English in the Elementary School.* (Englewood Cliffs, New Jersey: Prentice-Hall, Inc., 1967) for acquainting them with the quotations of George Bernard Shaw and the anonymous poet.

Despite obvious limitations, however, familiarity with phonics, and the ability to break up a word into parts are valuable skills when reading; they definitely make spelling attempts easier, and finally, they enable the writer to divide a word with a hyphen at the end of a line. To help you teach your child to accomplish these tasks we are going to discuss some of the basic facts about syllabication that you will need to know. The following definition by Arthur W. Heilman although too sophisticated for your child, will serve as your point of departure.

DEFINITION: A syllable is a vowel or group of letters containing a vowel sound which taken together form a pronounceable unit.[5]

[Note that the definition implies that a *vowel* (or a vowel sound such as "y") must be present for a linguistic unit to be a syllable. Furthermore, although two or more vowels may appear in a single syllable, only one vowel sound is pronounced.]

EXAMPLE: The first syllable in "beautiful," "beau," has three vowels but only one vowel sound: ū.

Many adults can divide words into syllables with no trouble, but have forgotten the rules that helped them learn how. We are now going to list some of these rules that you can gradually introduce to your child as the need to divide words presents itself. Examples, designed to help teach their application to spelling, follow each rule.

---

5. *Phonics in Perspective* (Columbus, Ohio: Charles E. Merrill Publishing Co., 1968), p. 77.

RULE I
Words can be divided into syllables between two like consonants.

EXAMPLES:

funny	fun-ny
balloon	bal-loon
rabbit	rab-bit
little	lit-tle
puzzle	puz-zle

EXERCISE:

Copy the example above and ask the child to point out the two consonants in the middle of each word that are the same. Explain the rule and point out how each word has been divided into syllables. Then have the child break apart the words below.

1. daddy
2. letter
3. merry
4. happy
5. sorry
6. pretty

RULE II
Words can be divided into syllables between unlike consonants unless those consonants represent a single sound.

EXAMPLES:

contest	con-test
carpet	car-pet
monkey	mon-key

Note that single speech sounds stay together:

fa-ther	("th" makes a single sound)
ta-ble	("bl" makes a single sound)
tur-tle	("tl" makes a single sound)

EXERCISE:
As in the exercise above, first use the example to illustrate the rule; then have the child break the following words apart:

1. candy (Note that the "y" serves as a vowel here)
2. after
3. party

RULE III
A single consonant between vowels usually goes with the second syllable.

EXAMPLES:
baby	ba-by
around	a round
water	wa-ter

EXERCISE:
After using the example to illustrate the rule, have the child break the following words apart:
1. alone (a-lone)
2. away (a-way)
3. today (to-day)
4. solo (so-lo)

RULE IV
Words are divided into syllables between two vowel sounds unless they represent a single sound. (Only teach this rule when the child is reading words as difficult as those in the examples.)

EXAMPLES:
create	cre-ate
theater	the-a-ter
idea	i-de-a

Note that single speech sounds stay together:

eat   (only the $\bar{\text{e}}$ is heard)
great   (only the $\bar{\text{a}}$ is heard)

In addition to the four rules above, certain principles govern the role endings play in a word's final syllable. Three follow:

1. The **ed** ending forms a final syllable when the root word ends with "d" or "t." (For example, need-ed, want-ed)
2. **ble, cle, dle, gle, kle, ple, tle,** and **vle** usually serve as the final syllables in words containing them. (In other words, "le" and the consonant before it constitutes the final syllable of a word.)
3. **es, er,** and **ing** normally add an extra syllable to a word.

Word Endings

Some of the hardest words for children to spell are those involving endings. Learning spelling rules for these endings can make things a lot easier.

Before the study of a spelling word is terminated, endings may be added to show the child other forms its spelling can take. Only add endings, however, when similar forms have already been introduced in previous spelling lessons. If the child has had the -**ing** ending on a word such as **go,** for example, but not on a word like **ride** (which must drop an **e** before adding the -**ing**), then do not show the child **riding** when you teach him to spell **ride.** Once **riding** or a similar word does appear in the child's spelling list, however, you should teach the principle involved (Principle #1 below) and may henceforth show him what the -**ing** form of a verb with a silent **e** at the end will look like.

To illustrate this, suppose **riding** appears in the child's spelling list. You would teach it like any other word using the teaching-learning and practice strategies detailed above. You should then teach Principle #1 dealing with the silent **e**. Thereafter, when a verb fitting that principle appears in the child's spelling list (such as "slide"), you will show him how to take off the **e** and add -**ing** (sliding).

Here is a list of other endings that may appear on spelling words:

-s or -es	-est
-ing	-ful
-ed	-fully
-er	-ly

PRINCIPLE #1

The silent e at the end of a word is dropped before an ending beginning with a vowel is added.

Example:	come	coming
	write	writing

(Note that **hope** becomes **hopeful.** The **e** is not dropped because the ending **-ful** does not begin with a vowel.)

PRINCIPLE #2

A one syllable word which ends with a consonant often doubles the consonant before adding an ending.

Example:	run	running
	get	getting

PRINCIPLE #3

Change the y to i before adding an ending.

Example:	lady	ladies
	cry	cries
	happy	happier, happiest, happily
	sky	skies
	baby	babies

Exception:	**If a vowel comes before the y it may stay the same.**

Example:	day	days
	boy	boys
	monkey	monkeys

PRINCIPLE #4
Spelling Plurals

Most nouns become plural by adding -s or -es. Instruct the child to listen to the way the word sounds. If the plural form sounds like it adds a new syllable to the word, spell it with -es unless the word ends in a vowel.

Example: **dishes** and **faces** both sound like the plural forms a new syllable. Add **-es** to dish, but face already ends in a vowel *(e)* so just add **-s**.

RULE I.
Add -es after s, sh, ch, z, and x.

EXAMPLE:
  bus-buses
  dish-dishes
  church-churches
  buzz-buzzes
  fox-foxes

EXERCISE:
Have the following words copied and made plural.

  kiss
  wash
  peach
  box
  six
  fizz

RULE II.
Add -s in most other cases (after all other consonants, after all vowels, and even when the plural has a z sound).

EXAMPLE:
dog-dogs
stove-stoves
bird-birds
house-houses

EXERCISE:
Copy these words and make them plural.

show
chicken
town
toy
rope
race

RULE III.
Some words form the plural without adding -s.

(About the only way to learn these words is to treat each individually as it comes up in a list.)

EXAMPLES:

mouse	— mice
man	— men
woman	— women
tooth	— teeth
goose	— geese
fish	— fish*
deer	— deer*
sheep	— sheep*

*The plural is identical to the singular.

PRINCIPLE #5:
Most nouns ending in -f or -fe become plural by changing this ending to -v and adding -es.

EXAMPLE:

calf	— calves
leaf	— leaves
half	— halves
loaf	— loaves
elf	— elves
hoof	— hooves
shelf	— shelves
wife	— wives
life	— lives
knife	— knives

SPELLING LAWS

The following two statements are *always* true, thus deserve to be called laws:

LAW #1
The letter q is always followed by u.

EXAMPLE:
queen
quick
quiet

LAW #2
I before e, except after c and except when together they sound like long a.

EXAMPLE:
piece
believe
field

after c: receive

sound like long a: neighbor
weigh

Homonyms

Homonyms are words that sound alike but are spelled differently and have different meanings (for example, *there* and *their*). They present no real problem in reading where their meanings are clear from the context, but in writing the child often forgets which spelling goes with the word he needs.

We believe homonyms should be taught as they come up naturally, either in a spelling list or in the child's writing. When only one half of a homonym pair appears, teach it alone, making sure that the child knows its meaning, and leave its counterpart for later. To teach them together is artificial and may only result in the child's confusing the two more than he would normally.

When the second word's time does come, teach it as a completely different word with a different meaning and spelling. At that time you may show the two words together and use a homonym exercise similar to the model suggested below. Encourage the child to play a game with you by making up sentences using both words.

For example, suppose the words in question were:

by-buy   see-sea   week-weak

The child could be presented with the following sentences and asked to fill in the blanks. Afterward the two of you might make up others.

A _____ has seven days.

The _____ water is salty.

The sick boy was _____.

He drove _____ our house.

Can you _____ the sunset?

I may _____ that book.

rode-road   plain-plane   tied-tide

He _____ down the _____.
The _____ landed.
He _____ up the boat at high _____.
The house was in _____ view.

Or to simply teach one pair at a time:

routes—roots

He mapped out the _____ we were to take.
A plant gets it food through its _____.

peace—piece

He ate a _____ of pie.
The two countries signed the _____ treaty.

eight—ate

Tom ran _____ miles.
I _____ an apple.

Here is a list of some common homonyms that you may encounter in your teaching. Undoubtedly, you will be able to add to the collection.

I'll	— aisle, isle
won	— one
sense	— cents
to	— two, too
I	— eye, aye
by	— buy
sea	— see
week	— weak
break	— brake
rode	— road
plain	— plane
tied	— tide
weight	— wait
route	— root
piece	— peace
beet	— beat
rain	— reign
know	— no
knew	— new, gnu
knot	— not
son	— sun
great	— grate
would	— wood
read	— reed
be	— bee
tail	— tale
sight	— site
here	— hear
there	— their
our	— hour

Contractions

Contractions are used quite frequently in speech, hence will appear in your child's writing vocabulary as well. As they do come up, either in his reading or writing, you can talk about them as being a short way to write two words by combining them into one. Explain that the apostrophe takes the place of the missing letters.

A first step toward learning to spell contractions is to play a matching game in which those the child needs to study are written in one column and their two word equivalents (in mixed up order) in another. The child can then match the proper pairs by drawing lines between them.

A variation of this exercise consists of a card game for two in which a separate index card is made for each contraction and for each two-word equivalent. The cards are mixed up and half dealt to each player. The two players then take turns asking the other for the match he needs. For example, if the child has "I'll" he must ask you for "I will." Any pair in his hand, or which he achieves through asking, may be put down. When all cards are matched into pairs, the game is over. (Once a good number of contractions are known, the game can include a deck of cards that the players draw from, as in the well-known game, "Go Fish.")

Here is a list of contractions that the child is likely to encounter by the time he finishes the sixth grade in school:

aren't	are not	I'm	I am
can't	cannot	isn't	is not
couldn't	could not	it's	it is
didn't	did not	I've	I have
doesn't	does not	she's	she is
don't	do not	they're	they are
hadn't	had not	there's	there is
haven't	have not	wasn't	was not
here's	here is	we'll	we will
he's	he is	weren't	were not
I'd	I would	we've	we have
I'll	I will	you're	you are

As always, we recommend that you do not teach the spellings of contractions until the need arises. It is more important that the child can read than spell them, since the two-word counterpart can almost always be used equally well, and is often superior, in writing.

Special Problems Related to Learning to Spell

The Problem. Some adults who are able to achieve quite adequately in their careers never learned to spell. Spelling requires the individual to possess four rather easily defined skills, the absence of any one of which can create a poor speller. They are:

1. the ability to hear sounds accurately,
2. a good knowledge of phonics (or the ability to match letters to sounds),
3. a good memory for words with irregular spellings, and
4. a reasonable fluency in handwriting.

There are ways to compensate for poor spelling, such as the use of a dictionary or the presence of a dictaphone and a good secretary. Usually things are not this simple, however. An individual must have *some* spelling skills just to locate a word in a dictionary and very few children have dictaphones and secretaries to get them through the many years of written assignments in school. It is, therefore, necessary to find ways to help the child who does have difficulty at his current stage of development and plan for his future. To do this, you must think in terms of either correcting the problem or finding some way to get around it through alternate spelling strategies. First, however, it is necessary to pinpoint the problem. Here are some questions which may help.

1. *Is the child's hearing accurate?* Does he always answer when you call him from another room? Are his answers appropriate to your questions or could he be mistaking one word for another that sounds similar? If you have any doubt at all about this, take him to be tested by an audiologist in a hospital clinic or ask your pediatrician to refer you to a doctor specializing in eyes, ears, and throat, called an otologist.

2. *Does the child have poor command of phonics?* Can he name some of the letters that stand for sounds within a word by listening to it? At the very least, he should be able to reproduce beginning consonant sounds and long vowels. (It is much easier to recognize sounds in reading than supply the letters they represent in spelling.)

3. *Does the child have trouble learning to spell words such as "people," "music," or "bicycle," but none with "tomato," "interest," or "farmer"?* The first three words are quite irregular while the final three are spelled pretty much the way they sound. If you notice a consistent pattern like this, your child may be having memorization trouble (or may be using a speller which emphasizes linguistic similarities to the exclusion of irregularities).

4. *Do you sometimes have to ask the child how he meant to spell a word because you can't make out his letters?* This shouldn't happen. By now his printing should at least be legible.

Recommendations. If the answer to any of the above questions is affirmative, here are some courses of action which you may wish to take.

1. **Hearing.** If the child has a hearing problem which cannot be corrected by a hearing aid, he may need special education. In any case, he must be trained to watch the speaker's mouth closely, a skill which is best facilitated by a speech therapist working with both parent and child. When it comes to spelling, he will have to rely more on memorization than children who can write words the way they sound.

2. **Phonics.** The child should, at a minimum, be instructed in the identification of the letters representing all the consonant sounds, blends, and long vowels. Phonics instruction does not guarantee spelling success, of course: many poor spellers are quite adept at sounding out their words. It is far rarer, however, to find a good speller who does not also have good phonics skills.

3. **Memorization.** Children who have trouble memorizing things should be guided through several different techniques until the one that works best is found. Try different amounts of emphasis on the various steps in the teaching-learning strategy and practice techniques, or try having the child spell the word aloud while writing it a few times for several consecutive days. You should also stress the importance of using the dictionary to check spellings.

4. **Writing.** If the child has a handwriting disability, teach him to spell orally as much as possible (by omitting the writing step in the teaching-learning strategy) while concentrating on the remedial writing steps suggested in Chapter Two (see Structured Writing).

Alternate Spelling Strategies

When, despite all your best efforts, spelling continues to be a major problem for your child, alternate strategies should be emphasized. Two which have already been discussed are the Children's Dictionary and the Word Box, both of which can be relied upon much more heavily in writing given sufficient encouragement. A third, more direct approach, involves a strategy which we call the *spelling recognition technique*.

The Spelling Recognition Technique. This procedure is designed to help children cope with unusual problems in learning to spell words. Its object is to train the child to recognize when a word is misspelled so he knows it either has to be checked in a dictionary or, in a pinch, with an adult.

Many children have no idea which words they may have misspelled. Adults, on the other hand, often have to write a word and look at it before they can be sure whether or not it is being spelled correctly, that is whether it *looks* right or wrong. It stands to reason, therefore, that if children can be taught this important skill, their writing should include significantly fewer misspelled words. That end is the purpose of the spelling recognition technique.

It should only be practiced with words that the child can read without hesitation or sounding out (that is, his sight vocabulary). If you haven't already done so, begin compiling a Word Box containing these words and encourage the child to practice reading the contents frequently.

Now, although he can read these sight words without difficulty, the child with a spelling problem will not be able to spell most of them. Your initial job will not be to teach him to spell them, but to teach him to recognize when he has spelled them incorrectly.

To begin ask the child to spell selected words as you dictate them. Administer this quiz in the same way you did the one in the teaching-learning strategy phase. Save the results for later, when the child is not around, and use the words missed as follows:

Type five sight words on a sheet of paper, putting some on the left side of the page, some in the middle, and all of them on the right. (It is preferable that this exercise be typed when possible, because seeing errors in type sometimes helps children recognize that they don't look right.) Here is an example of what the exercise sheet might look like:

	snow		snow
reading			reading
where			where
	are		are
	gone		gone

Next, fill in the blanks in the first and second columns with the incorrect spellings your child supplied on his test. (Actual examples of misspellings from his writing are also excellent sources.) The final exercise might look something like this:

1. sno	snow	snow
2. reading	reding	reading
3. where	ware	where
4. or	are	are
5. goon	gone	gone

To engage the child in this activity you should cover up the third column in which all the words are correct with a large card or folded paper. Say each word, use it in a sentence, and say it again. The child is then to circle the word that is spelled correctly in column one or two, then slide his shield down one space to expose the right answer and correct himself. If he is right, go on to the next word. If wrong, he must say the word, spell it aloud, and copy the correct spelling next to the third column.

If your child is a poor speller, you should have him perform one of these exercises daily. In each recognition training activity some words that were missed previously should be included. You should also keep updating the exercises with mistakes made in the child's ongoing writing experiences. To do this, of course, you will need to record his spelling errors as we have previously suggested with the ultimate objective of teaching your child to find, and correct, his own. (Remember to always use the *child's* errors—never invent an incorrect spelling for a word.)

A word has to be said about reading. Reading is very important to improving spelling ability. The more a child looks at a word in print, the more likely he is to recognize when he has spelled it incorrectly. Also, the more reading words you can add to the child's Word Box, the greater will be his resource in which to look up spellings and the closer he will be to using a dictionary.

Spelling Lists

The list shown below, is based on one of the most comprehensive, carefully constructed group of spelling words ever put together. It was compiled by Drs. Ernest Horn (whose classical work in spelling is without equal) and Ernest J. Ashbaugh almost fifty years ago, and is just as relevant to children's writing today as it was then.[6]

We suggest that you use the words in this list only as a supplement. Your first choice should be spelling words your child brings home from school *in combination with* words he frequently misspells in his everyday writing.

This list can be helpful, however, in deciding which words you should choose to work with from the many your child misspells in his compositions. It is also a valuable source of words for the parent who does not have access to a school speller. Toward that end, we have broken the list into increasingly difficult sections. The child who can read at a beginning second grade level is ready to start with I and proceed in order through the remaining eight sections.

---

6. This list has been adapted from *Progress in Spelling* (J. B. Lippincott Company, 1935) by E. Horn and E. J. Ashbaugh.

Modified Horn-Ashbaugh Spelling List

LEVEL I

a	glad	love	so	very
all	go	me	some	want
am	going	Miss	sorry	was
and	good	mother	street	we
are	got	my	thank	well
at	had	new	that	went
aunt	has	not	the	were
be	have	now	them	when
been	here	of	there	will
but	home	on	this	with
come	how	one	time	write
daddy	I	our	to	year
dear	in	play	today	you
did	is	school	too	your
fine	it	second	took	
for	letter	see	town	
from	like	she	two	
get	little	sick	uncle	

LEVEL II—PART A

any	cut	girls	much	tonight
at	day	grade	papa	tree
as	do	hard	said	trees
best	does	hat	saw	white
book	doing	hope	sent	wish
books	door	if	set	yes
boy	fast	know	show	yet
boys	feel	long	sister	
candy	few	make	rake	
car	fun	man	teacher	
Christmas	girl	miss	thought	

LEVEL II—PART B

about	children	grandma	merry	thank
again	cold	happy	out	too
bad	coming	him	playing	took
birthday	cousin	his	school	town
black	down	just	second	uncle
blue	father	live	sick	want
both	first	lot	sorry	were
brought	gone	mamma	street	year

LEVEL II—PART C

after	dress	it's	paper	tell
afternoon	Easter	last	party	their
ball	feet	lots	please	thing
been	five	made	pretty	third
better	four	making	put	three
big	from	many	read	till
box	gave	milk	reading	us
bring	give	more	red	water
came	go	morning	room	week
can	grandmother	next	sent	what
card	hear	nice	six	where
class	hot	off	snow	while
dog	house	old	stay	wood
doll	I'm	only	summer	wrote

LEVEL II—PART D

along	don't	I'll	picture	they
an	every	kind	played	things
away	face	let	presents	think
baby	fall	Miss	rain	told
because	fell	Mrs.	right	valentine
bed	friend	must	run	wanted
before	getting	name	say	weeks
by	going	night	says	work
can't	good	no	seen	working
cat	guess	or	sending	write
close	hand	other	still	writing
could	having	over	sure	would
cow	he	pair	than	yours
dinner	her	pencil	then	

LEVEL III—PART A

add	dollar	kiss	pair	sum
arm	dry	laugh	piano	sun
ask	dull	learn	plays	tea
ate	east	light	poor	Thanksgiving
Ave.	egg	line	raining	than
bag	eight	lovingly	reader	thought
barn	few	makes	real	times
bat	find	maybe	river	until
bird	floor	meet	rock	walk
blow	flower	mile	rose	wants
brown	fly	money	same	warm
cake	fourth	month	seven	weather
call	friend	move	song	west
cannot	front	nine	south	wet
cent	getting	noon	St.	who
city	gets	north	stand	whole
coat	head	number	start	wind
could	hello	numbers	stayed	winter
color	hen	ought	stop	word
country	into	page	street	years

LEVEL III—PART B

act	cute	ice	nights	sleep
address	done	king	nose	something
already	dressed	late	oil	step
also	drink	leg	park	store
always	drive	lesson	part	story
awful	each	lives	pick	sure
bath	eye	look	pin	tail
bet	eyes	may	place	talk
boat	fat	mean	pupil	thanks
bought	feed	meat	reads	these
break	feel	merry	report	toy
burn	fight	mine	ride	visit
busy	fish	miss	ring	wall
butter	fix	moved	rip	wanted
cap	funny	moving	save	wash
care	gets	mud	seat	way
chicken	getting	music	sell	while
Christmas	half	myself	ship	won
coal	Halloween	neck	short	yard
comes	having	need	sing	
cry	hurt	niece	sit	

LEVEL III—PART C

ago	didn't	knew	piece	sweet
almost	died	know	please	swim
alone	does	left	ran	table
another	doors	liked	ready	tall
anyway	dresses	looks	rest	teach
apple	ear	mad	riding	teacher's
asked	eat	men	road	test
aunt	else	mistake	roll	that's
band	end	months	rooms	Thursday
bank	enjoy	must	rug	trip
before	even	mouth	running	try
beg	far	named	sat	Tuesday
believe	feeling	needed	Saturday	under
Bill	fire	never	second	unless
bit	flag	news	seed	upon
broke	flowers	nothing	seeing	vacation
broken	found	not	sending	washing
brother	friends	on	sew	washed
called	full	older	shall	watch
cars	game	once	shoe	which
church	garden	orange	side	wished
class	glass	pass	spring	wait
clean	guess	passed	stick	wear
clock	hair	pen	stockings	why
cook	haven't	pencil	stove	worse
cooking	heard	people	sugar	
cousin	horse	picked	Sunday	
cream	I'm	pictures	supper	
dance	keep	pie	suppose	
			surely	

LEVEL III—PART D

across	doctor	kitten	pile	stars
again	dogs	lady	pink	starts
answer	dolls	letters	plant	stores
anybody	don't	loving	pretty	study
anything	duck	meal	quit	such
arithmetic	eating	means	rag	tables
arms	eggs	met	reading	teacher
around	ends	midnight	recess	things
auntie	evening	might	ribbon	third
basket	everybody	mother's	rides	those
bags	everything	mumps	rings	tiny
beautiful	falls	nail	roads	top
because	farm	names	roses	toys
bedtime	first	near	sand	train
bee	fishing	nearly	says	uncle
bell	foot	nicely	seats	use
birds	forest	nuts	sewing	Wednesday
birthday	for	often	shoes	window
bread	forgot	only	shot	windows
brought	Friday	other	sides	woods
catch	games	others	since	wool
cents	good-by	own	singing	wore
chair	grandpa	pan	snowed	would
chickens	hate	papers	snowing	written
coming	hit	party	soap	wrote
cotton	horses	picture	sometime	yesterday
couldn't	isn't	pet	songs	
cows	its	pig	sorry	
desk	kindly	pigs	spelling	

7

Vocabulary Development

Words are the raw materials of writing. Children have four separate vocabularies that differ from one another substantially in size. The largest is their listening vocabulary comprised of words whose meanings they know when heard in conversation. Next comes their speaking vocabulary, then the reading vocabulary which in the good reader may eventually exceed the speaking vocabulary, and finally, bringing up the rear, is the set of words that can be used in written expression.

The goal for this chapter is to suggest some ways that this fourth vocabulary can be increased. The more words the child has at his disposal the easier it will be for him to express exactly what he wants to say which is, after all, the chief purpose of this book.

Ironically, the quickest way to do this is by working on the child's other three vocabularies. No one incorporates many words into his writing which he cannot understand, pronounce, *or* read!

The Listening and Speaking Vocabularies

Throughout your child's development you should take the time to both talk to him and answer his questions. Nothing you are doing at any given time is more important, so being too busy is simply not a good enough excuse.

Don't talk down to your child. Don't purposefully use a simpler vocabulary than you use in everyday conversation. Your child went from a listening vocabulary of *zero* to the point that he could understand practically everything said to him in a remarkably short time. Why should you ever try to arrest this surge? Use words in your everyday conversation which you know your child does not understand. He will either learn them through context clues or ask you what they mean.

Parents are familiar with the endless deluge of questions of the "What is that?" or "Why do. . . ?" genre. What they may not be aware of is that the child is really forcing them to expand his vocabulary while explaining the world around him at the same time. Hopefully you did not, or will not, allow your patience to wear too thin to continually answer these questions. Hopefully also you will not take the line of least resistance and give the shortest possible answer.

"What is that?"

"That is a truck" answers the question, but a better answer is:

"That is a truck. Trucks like that are used to haul food, clothing, and other things for us."

Such an answer will probably generate another question:

"What other things" or "What is 'haul'?" The parent who encourages such questions will have a far more verbal child than the parent who irritably discourages them. There is little doubt which type of parent is going to be reading this book, but it still doesn't hurt to be reminded of the importance of this everyday, sometimes annoying, occurrence. You should also remember that two can play the old questioning game. Ask your child what things are, what they are for, how they work, and so forth. Besides affording valuable verbalization exercise for the child, you may be surprised at how limited his vocabulary and understanding of the world around him really is. Identifying needs is one of the first steps in successful teaching.

You don't have to depend solely upon questions to expand vocabulary, however. It's enough to talk as you work around the house, drive to do errands, or shop in the supermarket. Talk about what you see along the road or street. Call attention to signs. Point out the beauties of nature.

As you do these things employ as varied and as descriptive a vocabulary as possible. In discussing natural phenomena, for example, think of the multitude of adjectives you can use in lieu of worn out words such as "pretty" or "nice": *bright* sunshine; *dark, fluffy,* or *white* clouds; *tall, green,* or *gigantic* trees; *white, deep,* or *wet* snow.

Buildings lend themselves to teaching concepts that children often find difficult: *tall, taller, tallest; narrow, wide, long.* Streets have things on the *left, right, straight ahead,* or on the *corner.* When shopping one must go *in* the store; look *on, over, behind,* or *next to* the counter; *under* or *over* the shelf; *between* two products; and look for *some,* a *few, several* or *many* things.

In other words, verbalize practically everything you do with your child. You will not be wasting time; you will be teaching him valuable words and relationships between words which he will be able to use in his writing.

Reading to your child. Some of our readers undoubtedly wonder why we don't eventually get tired of extolling the virtues of reading to children. The reason is that we don't know of anything more beneficial to their long-term intellectual development. Besides the pure unadulterated entertainment oral reading provides, besides its value in cementing a lasting bond between parent and child, and besides its proven value in helping children learn, oral reading is one of the best ways we know to increase the listening and, ultimately, the writing vocabularies.

We discussed reading to your child in some detail in our previous book. Here it is enough to say that you should read regularly to your child, making it a family activity long after everyone has begun to read on his own. Try to budget a half hour *everyday* even if (or perhaps we should say, especially if) it requires watching one less 30-minute situation comedy on television.

Read things the child enjoys, but don't hesitate to try to introduce different types of experiences. It isn't necessary to "read down" to a child; many can appreciate relatively advanced materials, but there is a fine line here. You will very quickly know if a book or story is too difficult by observing fidgeting and loss of interest. Vary your voice to fit the passage. Use a gruff voice for villains, a soft voice for mothers, and childlike voices for young people. Use an eerie voice or a whisper for scary passages; read faster and louder for action-packed scenes. In other words, "ham it up." Remember that you are not dealing with an adult who will judge your performance by professional standards. You are dealing with a child who will love every minute of it.

You don't have to read difficult material to increase your child's vocabulary. We suggest only that you not be afraid to try out new and stimulating books and stories periodically, but don't worry if your child develops his own distinctive tastes and demands that you cater to them. Even the simplest stories often contain a wealth of new words not yet in most children's vocabularies. The trick is to recognize them and point them out to the child. It is far too easy to assume that the meaning of relatively common words are understood because the sentences in which the words are embedded appear to be understood. The reason for this is that children learn very early to attend to the context in which unfamiliar words appear, thereby understanding the gist of the situation without knowing all the words.

For the most extreme example of difficult words hiding undetected in children's literature you need go no further than common nursery rhymes. In

> **Little Miss Muffet**
> **Sat on a** *tuffet*
> **Eating her** *curds* **and** *whey.*

how many children know what a tuffet is? How many parents, for that matter? Other examples abound. Many modern-day children probably don't know what *cinders* are in

> **Little Polly Flinders**
> **Sat among the cinders . . .**

The same is true of

> **Goosey, goosey** *gander,*
> *Whither* **shall I** *wander.*

Neither the rhyming words nor "whither" are likely to be understood, but the child, entranced by the rhyme and rhythm, is not likely to say anything. Ask the child if he knows what a *cinder* is. Tell him that a *gander* is a male (daddy) goose, that *whither* is very similar in meaning to *where*, that *wander* means *go* or *travel.*

It isn't always a good idea for the reader to interrupt the flow of a story, however, to teach the child the meaning of a word. Simply make a note of any words in a passage (along with their location) that are probably not understood. Then, after your reading session, or at another time altogether, you may read the sentence containing the word and ask the meaning.

Don't expect sophisticated definitions. You should be able to ascertain whether or not the meaning of a word is really known. If not, explain it in very simple terms, using words the child does know or help him look it up in his dictionary. If the child is too young to be able to use a dictionary effectively, it doesn't hurt for you to look the word up in front of him and read the definition. This will demonstrate that the dictionary is a useful, "grown-up" tool; it will also gradually teach him how to use one on his own.

Like everything, it is possible to have too much of a good thing. Developing a good vocabulary is a long-term, life-long project. You're not going to do anything overnight; attempting to do so will only turn the child off to words by subverting the real purposes of reading. Encourage the child to ask questions about unfamiliar words. Approach the teaching of words in a lighthearted, fun-oriented way. The key is persistence, not intensity.

If you were to teach one new word per day, for example, think what a difference it would make in intellectual development in a three-year span. A child who knows 1000 more words than his peers will have an unbelievable advantage both in school and in standardized test performance. So will the child who knows 200 or 300 more words. More importantly, both children will be able to express themselves more easily and more richly in writing.

The Reading Vocabulary

Once the child begins to read he will automatically add a great many words to his writing vocabulary. At first he will find few words that are not already in his spoken vocabulary, but the process of seeing words over and over again in print will encourage their use in writing. (This transition will be greatly facilitated if some help is provided in their spelling as discussed in Chapter Six.)

Reading is so relevant to the development of writing skills that it really doesn't make a lot of sense to discuss one without the other. The non-reader will be a non-writer as well. The child who does not enjoy reading will not enjoy writing.

The child who has been read to, talked with, and encouraged to read widely will usually develop a genuine love for reading. At first this love will include anything which can be read fluently. In the beginning children prefer to read orally when an adult or older child is willing to listen. Oral reading is especially useful for teaching the child new words since you can usually tell by the expression in his voice whether or not he understands the meaning. A discussion of the story will clarify this even further.

Later the child will learn to appreciate the advantage of reading silently while at the same time becoming more selective with respect to the topics he chooses. "Specializing" in one particular subject and reading only books that pertain to it is not at all uncommon. Some parents become sincerely concerned when a daughter refuses to read anything except horse stories, for example, or a son wants nothing that does not deal with automobile racing. Actually, nothing could be more natural or beneficial to the child's reading (and hence vocabulary) advancement. A child who becomes fervently interested in something will read two or three times as much as he did before the "bug" bit him and, although the new words encountered in the process may seem a little specialized, they will be readily transferable to other areas of study later on.

Silent, unsupervised reading does present a special problem with respect to vocabulary development, however. In nine cases out of ten, the child will not ask an adult the meaning of an unknown word, thus impeding the rate at which new words are added to his vocabulary. This practice can be arrested in one of two ways:

1. The child can be encouraged to copy each new word he encounters while reading silently. We have found that this works especially well when a bounty is paid (for example, a penny apiece). Later, parent and child can look the words up in a dictionary or, if the child isn't yet up to that, you can go over the meanings of each word with him. Leaving the child to look the words up on his own may put too much of a burden on his leisure time.
2. You can skim some of the materials your child is reading yourself, jotting down words which you suspect are not fully understood. Later, after the book is finished you can ask the child the meanings of the suspected words, teaching those which he indeed does not know.

The Writing Vocabulary

Knowing the meaning of a word when it is heard in a conversation or read in a sentence does not imply the ability to incorporate it in written communication. The best way to insure at least the capability for written utilization is to actually have a sentence constructed using the word in question.

You may be surprised at how difficult this task is for many children. A child can be told that a cinder is a piece of something that is almost completely burned, and he will seem to understand. If asked to write a sentence using the word *cinder*, however, you may be rewarded with a blank stare or something like:

Cinders are pretty.

You, of course, can never be satisfied with a sentence in which practically any noun is interchangeable. If a sentence cannot be written (or dictated if the child is not advanced enough to print), discuss the word further. Read the sentence or paragraph in which it was first encountered and explain its meaning as directly related to that context. You might even write an appropriate sentence yourself to prime the child's imagination. Words that are not yet in the listening or speaking vocabulary must be worked with before they have a chance of becoming part of his writing and even then they will require some additional priming before you expect to see them nestled in a composition.

Some method of increasing the visibility or profile of new words, therefore, must be found before their writing utilization can be assured. One way to do this is either to make sure that the child can spell the word or that it is conveniently listed somewhere that he can find it when the need arises. Being able to use a dictionary will be a great help in this respect, of course, but it will hardly help him recall the word if it's not on the tip of his tongue nor find it unless he has a fairly good idea of the word's spelling.

The Thesaurus. The answer for a mature writer lies in a thesaurus. All the writer need be able to do is to think of and spell a synonym. Once the child understands how to use the dictionary he too can be introduced to this aid. *In Other Words: A Beginning*

Thesaurus by A. Schiller and W. A. Jenkins (Lothrop, Lee, and Shepard Co.), for example, contains over 1000 synonyms for the 100 words most commonly used by children, uses informal language, and is illustrated with colorful pictures and photographs throughout.

Although nothing is really superior to a good thesaurus for increasing the writing vocabulary of intermediate level and advanced writers, beginners do not have the reading ability nor vocabulary comprehension to use something this sophisticated. What such a child can do, therefore, is construct his own! It can take any form, from a variation of the picture dictionary to a system of large index cards alphabetized by known words, with their new synonyms and sentences underneath. Have the child start with a simple list of new words encountered while reading or being read to, complete with synonyms and sentences (preferably his own— see First Stage). Then, as the list becomes unwieldy, the words can be classified, such as action words, words that describe things, names of animals, games, things that give rides, things to eat, noises, and so forth (see Second Stage).

First Stage: simple list, one word per card
                synonyms are very general

          <u>walk</u>   I walk to school.
           go

Second Stage: classifying cards divide the simple list into groups. Each word is written on a card as in the First Stage with an accompanying sentence and synonym. Here are some suggested classifiers and words to follow:

CLASSIFIER: **Things We Do:**
walk, go, run, play, work, fly, wash, drive, talk, kiss, ride, laugh, write, eat, sing, fish, . . .

CLASSIFIER: **Names of Animals:**
cat, dog, rabbit, bird, hen, horse, chicken, bee, cow, duck, pig, kitten, . . .

CLASSIFIER: **Things That Give Rides**
car, truck, bike, train, skates, sled, . . .

CLASSIFIER: **Family Members:**
mother, father, sister, brother, cousin, uncle, aunt, grandpa, grandma, . . .

CLASSIFIER: **What Size Is It?**
little, big, tiny, small, enormous, huge, gigantic, miniscule, . . .

CLASSIFIER: **Colors:**
white, black, blue, brown, green, red, orange, pink, . . .

CLASSIFIER: **How Someone Might Feel:**
happy, sad, cheerful, depressed, sick, fine, angry, puzzled, irritable, . . .

Third Stage: Synonyms become more descriptive. Each card now has a word with a list of synonyms, as in
walk: stride, stroll, strut, waddle, creep, limp
talk: whisper, shout, scream, speak, argue, persuade

A homemade thesaurus may also help to exorcise slang words from your child's writing. Enlist his help in compiling a list of substitutes. Suppose the word "dumb" is used indiscriminately, as with

I saw a dumb movie on T.V. last night.
Mary is dumb.
That birthday party was dumb.

Discuss other ways of describing a movie. Was it boring? Was it silly? Was the acting poor? The plot far-fetched? Could it be better described as uninteresting, better suited for "little kids," or did the child really enjoy the movie and is he just trying to say that it was funny? You will probably be astounded at the wide range of emotions and adjectives that can be attributed to one favorite word, at least until you stop to think how many meanings the word "cool" used to have for you.

The child's own thesaurus, then, can serve a dual function. It can expand his writing vocabulary as well as help make descriptions more precise and informative.

Vocabulary games. Expanding your child's vocabulary doesn't have to involve formal teaching 100 percent of the time. Children love playing verbal games with peers and grown-ups. Four which we consider especially valuable follow:

1. **Crossword puzzles.** Crossword puzzles are lots of fun. Few activities are more helpful in vocabulary building, partly because the child is forced to complete sentences or supply synonyms, partly because he receives immediate feedback following the activity. Books of children's puzzles are available but you will probably find constructing your own more useful since you can include words that your child knows, needs work on, or needs to learn. Below is an example of the type you might construct. (Keep the answers to the puzzles on a separate sheet of paper; the temptation to "peek" may be too great. If the child gets stuck, give him one answer at a time, seeing if he can complete the puzzle each time.)

C	L	O	W	N
O				E
A				E
T	I	R	E	D

ACROSS

1. Ronald MacDonald is a

   _____.

3. Someone who needs to take a nap is very _____.

DOWN

1. Something you wear when it is cold outside.

2. When you must have something, you _____ it. The answer rhymes with "feed."

Don't worry about elaborate interlocking lines and columns. Your main objective is to give the child practice in using and thinking about words.

We do suggest, however, that your clues be written in complete sentences and that you choose words with which you feel the child needs practice. For example, you could construct an entire puzzle using adverbs:

The boys ran _____.   (swiftly)

The mother whispered _____.   (softly)

The dog barked _____.   (loudly)

2. **Scrabble.** This is a fascinating game for people of all ages. You might think about occasionally playing special games with the young child where all opponents only use very simple three or four letter words. Generally speaking, however, you should include the child in regular adult games whenever possible because seeing words older siblings and parents know will both increase his vocabulary and motivate him to want to increase it. Be sure to explain the meaning of all words not understood and help formulate one when he appears stuck. Depending upon the child's personality, you can devise a special point system for him, allow him to have more word blanks, or simply let him exchange any letters he does not want. Having the child play with someone else as a team is an especially good idea.

3. **Twenty Questions.** This old word game has been popular since it appeared on television years ago. It still remains a good way to pass the time on trips. For those of you who don't remember how it is played, one player thinks of a word (proper nouns are excluded), and the others have a total of 20 questions to guess its exact identity. To be legal each question must be answerable with a simple "yes" or "no," after the initial question of "animal, vegetable, or mineral" is answered. What the game does is force the player to focus on specific properties of a word, categories to which it does and does not belong, as well as similarities and differences between it and other words.

4. **What is a** _____. This game[1] is specifically designed to force the player to attend to visual and functional characteristics of common objects and, above all, to use precise language in describing them. To begin, one player picks out an object (perhaps something in the room, something with wheels, or

---

1. This game has been adapted from a classroom exercise discussed by Dr. Paul R. Daniels in one of his graduate courses for teachers at The Johns Hopkins University.

anything else that is agreed upon in advance) and asks the player to his left to describe it without using its name. The person whose turn it is to describe then writes (or dictates if he is too young) the best definition he can think of in as few words as possible (but always using complete sentences). When he is finished each player tries to find fault with the definition by thinking of another object or word to which it could apply. If no one mounts a successful challenge, the original player receives five points. Each player who does think of an exception, however, and is able to amend the original definition accordingly, receives five points. After everyone has had a chance to both challenge and amend the definition, all players attempt to write a final version in as few words as possible. Five points are awarded to the writer using the fewest words who both includes all the amendments and uses complete sentences.

To illustrate how this game might proceed, suppose the child's task was to describe a chair. A very good start might be "A chair is something with four legs that you sit on." The second player could object to this description, however, by saying that so is a bench. This player must then do something to exclude benches so he adds, "It is only big enough for one person to sit on." Now this second sentence narrows the possibilities greatly, but it is possible someone else would object that what has been said so far applies to a stool as well, adding that "a chair also has a back to lean on." At this stage all the players might attempt to reformulate the definition incorporating the two earlier objections. Suppose one player defines a chair in the following precise manner:

> A chair is something with four legs that you sit on. It is only big enough for one person to sit on. It also has a back to lean on.

This player receives five points for the shortest definition still written in complete sentences. All points are tallied and the game continues with another word and another player attempting to define it. Many variations of this game are possible, including forcing all responses to be in writing. Here one person assigns everybody the same word and reads each response, writing objections or exceptions to force more precise descriptions. All definitions are read at the end of the game and points tallied.

Word games are as much fun as they are instructive. It is truly difficult in this age of television entertainment to set aside some time each evening for intellectual games or a family hour of reading and writing. Yet parents who are disheartened by declining achievement levels in the children of this nation must take the initiative to do so.

FORMAL WORD STUDY

As effective as games are for building vocabulary, young writers need more concentrated work with words as well. We suggest some formal work in vocabulary development as an adjunct to the child's actual writing sessions. The remainder of this chapter will deal with the teaching of word relationships and characteristics that can give the child a wider range of experience using and playing with words.

Synonyms

Synonyms are words that have the same or nearly the same meaning. We have discussed improving writing by replacing bland, over-used words with more precise, descriptive ones. Synonyms, however, involve a more subtle gradient of distinction. Here the classification is limited to words that express the same idea. When you persuade your child to write about a *boring* rather than a *dumb* movie you are not really dealing with equivalent meanings. When you define "boring" with the word *uninteresting,* on the other hand, you have selected a synonym.

Synonyms expand the writing vocabulary while imparting a clearer understanding of words already in it. The teaching of synonyms is quite straightforward. You start with the child's word, proceed to a word substitute, then use the substitute in the child's original sentence.

To begin, search through your child's writing for suitable words. For a word to qualify there should be another word in his listening vocabulary that means nearly the same thing. Below is an example of a list you might start to keep:

Word Found in Child's Writing	Synonym
tall	high
say	speak (talk)
yell	shout
nice	kind
rock	stone
bang	crash
throw	toss
run	dash
begin	start
scare	frighten
big	huge (enormous)

Read each pair of words and discuss their meanings, then take sentences from the child's own writings and copy them using the synonyms as seen below. After a sentence is completed in this way, have the child read both options and discuss their meanings. (When the child's sentences are not useful, construct new ones.)

The boy climbed the tall (high) fence.

Did he talk (speak) to you?

Don't yell (shout)!

That rock (stone) came from the mountain.

The loud noise scared (frightened) me.

As soon as the ball is thrown he will run (dash) to second base.

The dog was big (huge).

Ask if there is a difference between a big and a huge (or enormous) dog; is one bigger than the other? How about running versus dashing? talking versus speaking?

You should never be at a loss for words to use if your child writes regularly. Once a word is incorporated into his writing, you may include it in the left hand column above and find another synonym for the right hand column.

Other sources of words may be found in the child's reading. You may even show him a list of words in need of synonyms so that the child can be on the lookout for suitable candidates. As he comes across unusual words which he thinks can be used in place of old familiar ones, he can (1) use his dictionary to check out the hunch, (2) try substituting the old word for the new one in a sentence, or

(3) simply ask you if the two words are synonyms. If the child conscientiously pursues this line of inquiry, he will soon realize that even though almost every word has *many* synonyms there are different shades of meanings involved in each.

Another exercise that will get the child to think of synonyms is a story with blanks to be filled in. These can be made from scratch or a paragraph can be copied from a book you think your child could read. In place of certain nouns, verbs, adjectives, and adverbs, leave blanks. The child then reads the sentences filling in the blanks so that they make sense. Do not worry about correct spellings. A second reading can also be undertaken in which the blanks can be filled in again using different words. Here is an example.

Pam went to the zoo. She rode with

father in the _____. They _____

on the way. At the zoo Pam saw _____.

They were big and _____. They could

run _____. Pam laughed and said, "I

want to come back _____."

The six blanks could be filled with many different words. For example:

1. car, truck, train
2. talked, sang, slept
3. tigers, elephants, bears
4. orange, grey, brown
5. fast, quickly, slowly
6. soon, tomorrow, later

Opposites (Antonyms)

Many words have counterparts that mean just the opposite. The ability to identify these pairs or antonyms helps increase vocabulary, enrich, and lend precision to written expression.

Consider the following list as an example.

tall	short
all	none
front	back
first	last
large	small
boy	girl
man	woman
crooked	straight
shout	whisper
pull	push
praise	blame
clean	dirty
same	different
hard	soft
easy	difficult
thick	thin
fat	skinny
simple	complicated
agree	argue
happy	sad
weak	strong
cool	warm
cold	hot
far	near
lost	found
north	south
rough	smooth

These word pairs can be treated and compiled in exactly the same way as were the synonym lists, with meanings being discussed and words substituted within sentences. Children often enjoy this latter activity because they can turn the meaning of an entire sentence around by changing only one word.

I <u>lost</u> (found) my ball.

That child is a <u>boy</u> (girl).

My dress is <u>clean</u> (dirty).

There are any number of exercises that you can construct with word similarities and differences, all of which are profitable if they simply induce the child to think about, play with, or manipulate *words*. You could, for example, construct three columns as follows with the first containing familiar words, the second synonyms in mixed-up order, and the third antonyms in mixed-up order. The child then connects appropriate words in each column with lines:

Word Used in Writing	Synonym	Antonym
happy	delicate	wet
dry	everything	sad
all	aid	harm
soft	parched	none
help	cheerful	coarse

To make things more difficult the child could be responsible for supplying the synonyms and antonyms.

Word Used in Writing	Synonym	Antonym
big	_____	_____
beautiful	_____	_____
dead	_____	_____
crooked	_____	_____
etc.		

Multiple Meanings

It can be confusing to hear the same word used in several different ways. When a familiar word comes up in a new context, point out that one word may have two or more completely different meanings while retaining the same spelling and pronunciation. The only way to tell its meaning is to see how it is used in a sentence.

Sentences which illustrate this phenomenon are fun to read.

My sick friend is not well.
The water came from the well.
Well, well, what will she do next?

The children played on the slide.
We saw a slide with horses on it. (via a film projector)
If you walk on ice you may slide.

The child can make up similar sentences to illustrate multiple meanings as they are encountered. A few of the possibilities are:

hide —the skin of an animal and what one does to keep from being found.
pet —an animal and how you touch an animal.
fly —an insect and what that insect does.
right—a direction and what your mother always is
train—something to ride on and something you try to do to your pets
tire —the round things on cars and what you do as you work.
fire, light, leaves, mean, saw, can, and a cast of many more

Heteronyms

Heteronyms are words that are spelled the same but have both different meanings and pronunciations. We don't suggest that you make a special point of teaching these words, only that you point out their existence and the individual meanings and pronunciations as they are encountered. Here are a few; undoubtedly you will be able to think of many more:

separate	(sep′ə -rāt)	vs	(sep′ĕr-it)
tear	(târ)	vs	(têr)
lead	(lēd)	vs	(led)
read	(rēd)	vs	(red)
live	(līv)	vs	(liv)
wound	(wound)	vs	(wōōnd)
subject	(sub′jikt)	vs	(səb-jekt′)
rebel	(reb′il)	vs	(re-bel′)
content	(kən-tent′)	vs	(kon′tent)
entrance	(en′trəns)	vs	(in-trans′)
bow	(bō)	vs	(bou)
present	(prez′ nt)	vs	(pri-zent′)

(Webster's New World Dictionary of the American Language: College Edition)

Prefixes

Russell G. Stauffer[2] once did a study of Edward L. Thorndike's list of 30,000 common words used in children's and adults' literature and found that almost 20 percent of them employed one of fifteen prefixes. These and other common prefixes follow:

ab	- from	(abdomen)
ad	- to	(admit)
be	- by	(beside)
com	- with	(companion)
de	- from	(detour)
dis	- apart, not	(displace)
en	- in	(entrap)
ex	- out	(exclaim)
im	- in	(imbibe)
in	- not	(inactive)
mis	- wrong	(misplace)
non	- not	(nonsence)
pre	- before	(predetermined)
pro	- ahead of	(proceed)
re	- back, again	(replay)
sub	- under	(submarine)
un	- when attached to verbs it indicates a reversal of the verb's action (undo)	
	when attached to nouns or adjectives it means *not* (un-pleasant)	

Unfortunately, as the examples indicate, most of these prefixes will not help the child to either unravel a word's *meaning or* add it to his writing vocabulary. Exceptions are perhaps **re-** (especially its **again** meaning), **un-**, and for the older child perhaps **pre-, non-, sub-,** and **dis-.**

When teaching prefixes, explain that they are certain letters found at the beginning of many words and that they carry a certain meaning. Illustrate this concept with familiar words.

---

2. Russell G. Stauffer, "A study of Prefixes in the Thorndike List to Establish a List of Prefixes That Should Be Taught in the Elementary School." (*Journal of Educational Research,* XXXV, 1942, p. 453-458).

For example, you might explain that **un** on the front of a word usually means **not:**

unhappy	un + happy	(not happy)
unknown	un + known	(not known)
unkind	un + kind	(not kind)
unable	un + able	(not able)
unafraid	un + afraid	(not afraid)
unlocked	un + locked	(not locked)

You can then point out some new words which begin with **un** and ask the child to guess their meaning, such as *unasked, unfasten, unending, unworn, untwisted,* and so forth. (Always use words which retain their complete spelling following the prefix.)

Again we must warn you that this sort of exercise will be over children's heads if applied to most common prefixes. The only ones we can recommend are **re-, non-, un-** and possibly (but to a lesser extent), **sub-, pre-,** and **dis-.**

Conclusion

We have by no means exhausted all the alternatives available to parents wishing to expand their children's vocabularies. We have not even mentioned the use of metaphor ("The moon was a ghostly galleon . . ."), simile ("lips *like* wild strawberries"), expressions ("beating around the bush"), or a dozen other useful strategies and tools.

You now have a starting point, however, and a blueprint for action to use with the *beginning* writer. Vocabulary development, like spelling, is an open-ended process that is never completed, never mastered. The best you can hope to do is to ignite your child's curiosity about words, the building blocks of our language, and show him how to satisfy that curiosity. If you accomplish that, and if you continue to encourage him to write and read as part of his lifestyle, then you will have done all you can and should do as a language teacher.

8

Punctuation, Paragraph, and Dictionary Skills

Most of the skills taught in this chapter have been introduced previously in one form or another. Your child has learned to place periods and question marks at the end of sentences in Chapter Five, to use a picture dictionary in Chapter Three, and to write in paragraphs (without indenting them) in Chapter Four. These skills will now be extended to more advanced applications which, by the time they are mastered, will give the young writer almost all the basic tools he needs.

Punctuation

ACTIVITY #1
Punctuating Sentences

Although sentences always begin with capital letters, they may end with any of three types of punctuation. Sentences that tell something end in periods, whether they are basically statements (called declarative sentences) or commands (called imperative sentences). Those which ask questions (interrogative sentences) end with question marks while exclamatory sentences (that is, those which show surprise) are punctuated with exclamation marks.

Remind the child what a sentence is (a group of words expressing a complete thought), and talk about the three different ways that they can be punctuated using the examples below. When you feel these concepts are understood administer Exercise 8-1. Examples of correctly punctuated sentences from the child's past writing can be used for additional practice.

Sentences That Tell. Sentences that tell us something fall into two groups: those that make statements and those that give commands or orders.

EXAMPLES: *Statements*   *Commands*
He is my friend.   Close the door.
I know how to write.   Look at the sign.

Sentences That Ask. Ask the child if he remembers how sentences that ask questions end. If he answers "with question marks," compliment him. If not, remind him.

EXAMPLES: Who is that?
Can you hear the music?
Do you want to go?

Sentences That Show Surprise or Excitement. Undoubtedly the child will have encountered exclamation marks in his reading. Many comics, in fact, seem to use them in place of periods. Explain that their purpose is to communicate surprise or excitement to the reader. Read sentences containing them with excitement in your voice.

EXAMPLES: There's Santa Claus!
My hand hurts!

Exercise 8-1
Copy these sentences in large print and read each one with your child before having the exercise completed. Sentence 3 and 7

should be read with excitement. Give the following directions: *These sentences have mistakes. They are missing capital letters and punctuation marks. Circle the letters that should be capitalized and put in the missing punctuation marks.*

1. this is an interesting book
2. who is that
3. the boys are in a big fight
4. can you come with me
5. what is your name
6. he went fishing
7. i got really scared
8. do you go to school
9. my dog is black and white
10. will you be my friend

ACTIVITY #2
Capitalization

The child has already learned that sentences begin with capital letters. It is now time to introduce other situations that require capitalization. As with punctuation, you should first explain the principle, demonstrate with a few examples, and reinforce the concepts with both Exercise 8-2 and examples from your child's own writing. Also, from now on when the child forgets to capitalize in his writing, remind him of this lesson.

EXAMPLES:

FIRST NAMES: John, Mary, Tom, Ann, (the child's name)

LAST NAMES: Jones, Smith, Robinson, (your last name)

TITLES: Miss Martin, Mr. Long, Mrs. Smith, Captain John Smith, Aunt Jane (Mr. and Mrs. are abbreviations as well as titles.)

INITIALS: J. Smith (John Smith), R. A. Waters (Ruth Ann Waters), J. P. J. (John Paul Jones), (the child's initials)

STREETS: Main Street, Forest Drive, Maple Avenue, Rock Circle, (your street)

CITIES:	New York City, Boston, Milford, (your city or town)
STATES:	Florida, Delaware, (your state)
COUNTRIES:	United States of America, Canada
BUILDINGS:	Oak Tree School, Fat Boy Restaurant
OTHER PLACES:	Moon River, Atlantic Ocean, Hyde Park
NAMES ON THE CALENDAR:	Monday, Tuesday, Christmas, Hanukkah, Father's Day, January, February
MAIN WORDS IN TITLES:	(See Chapter Three)
PARTS OF LETTERS:	(See Chapter Four)
QUOTATIONS:	The first letter in a quotation begins with a capital letter, as in

John said, "Where is Bill?"

POETRY:	The first word in each line of a poem traditionally begins with a capital letter, as in

Whistle and you shall see
Nobody around but me.

Exercise 8-2

Copy the following exercise for your child to complete.

These sentences have words which are missing capital letters. Circle the letters that should be capitalized.

1. mary, jane, and i are friends.
2. My birthday is in january. (Note that birthday is not capitalized.)
3. Can you go monday?
4. Jack said, "may i please go too?"
5. Our favorite holiday is christmas and it comes in december.
6. mr. c. a. brown, captain bill markman, and miss kate white all came to visit.
7. dallas, dover, and dodge city are cities.
8. applegate school is on park street just below the rocky mountains.
9. My school is in this city. (Note that neither school nor city are capitalized because they do not serve as "proper" names.)

ACTIVITY #3
Other Uses of Periods

Now that the child is familiar with the most common use of the period in sentence punctuation, you may teach him three others.

Initials. An initial, that is the first letter of a person's name, is written as a capital letter and followed by a period.

EXAMPLES: See the examples under Activity #2.

Abbreviations. Abbreviations are established short forms for writing longer words. The fact that they are abbreviations and not words is denoted by the period that follows them.

EXAMPLES:

TITLES OF PEOPLE:	Mr. (Mister), Mrs. (Mistress), Dr. (Doctor), Rev. (Reverend), Jr. (Junior), Capt. (Captain), Gen. (General)
DAYS OF THE WEEK:	Mon. (Monday), Tues. (Tuesday)
MONTHS OF THE YEAR:	Jan. (January), Feb. (February)
NAMES OF PLACES:	R.I. (Rhode Island), Del. (Delaware), U.S. (United States), P.O. (Post Office), St. (Street), Av. (Avenue)
MEASURES:	lb. (pound), oz. (ounce), qt. (quart), doz. (dozen), ft. (foot/feet), in. (inch), yd. (yard), hr. (hour), cm. (centimeter), m. (meter), km. (kilometer), gr. (gram), mg. (milligram)

After Numerals. The period follows both Arabic or Roman numerals used in a list or outline, as in:

1.	or	I.
2.		II.
3.		III.

EXERCISE 8-3

These words and sentences are missing periods. Correct each one by putting in the periods.

1. R L Stevenson is my favorite author.
2 He came on Mon and stayed until Fri (Note the 2 needs a period.)
3. Boston, Mass is his home
4. Dr Brook came to see the baby
5 She bought one doz eggs, a qt of milk, and two ft of ribbon.
6 The house on Joy Av was sold

ACTIVITY #4
Commas

The child has encountered numerous commas through his reading. He was probably taught at that time that their function was to make the reader slow down or pause. Commas have other uses as well, such as helping to separate ideas or words to make them easier to understand. A few examples of this follow:

Dates. The comma separates the day of the month from the year, thus making the date easier to read.

EXAMPLES: January 2, 1980
September 14, 1981
November 11, 1942

Cities and States. The comma separates the name of the city from the name of the state in an address or sentence.

EXAMPLES: Newark, Delaware
Little Rock, Arkansas
Chicago, Illinois

Lists. Words in a series or list within a sentence are separated by commas. This can take the form of a comma following each word before the *and.* Also, the comma separates a series of adjectives which separately modify the same noun.

EXAMPLES: I can run, jump, hop, and dance.
Red, blue, green, and purple are colors.
The girl wore a long, yellow coat.

Yes/No. When responses of yes or no begin a sentence, they are usually followed by a comma.

EXAMPLES: Yes, I know that.
No, I can't go.

Direct Address. When the name of the person being addressed directly is placed in the sentence, it must be separated from the rest of the sentence by commas. One comma is used if the name is either the first or last word, two when it falls in the middle of the sentence.

EXAMPLE: John, come into the house.
Stop that noise, Mark.
Sit down, Jim, and read your letter.

Quotations. Direct reproductions of oral language are set off from the rest of the sentence by commas either following or preceding the quotation marks. (Note that commas or periods following direct quotes are placed inside the quotation marks.)

EXAMPLE: Bill said, "Come in."
"I will go," Tom replied.
(We assume that you have already taught the use of quotation marks in Chapter Four.)

Salutations. The name of the person to whom a personal letter is written is followed by a comma.

EXAMPLE: Dear Jack,
Dear Grandmother,

Closings. Commas follow words which signal the end of a letter and precede the correspondent's name.

EXAMPLE: Love,
Your friend,
Thank you,

EXERCISE 8-4

The following sentences are written without commas. Put the commas in where they belong.

1. "Come quickly" cried Sue.
2. Is that you Joe?
3. No I don't like that game.
4. The children put a hat scarf glasses and a belt on the snowman.
5. We live in Nashville Tennessee.
6. John was born on April 25 1974.
7. Mary stop that right now!
8. Bill moved from Baltimore Maryland on December 15 1974.
9. I like ice cream candy and sodas.
10. "Yes I'll go" said Judy.

Paragraphs

Although the word or the sentence is usually considered the primary building block in writing, some experts argue that it is really the paragraph which is the basic unit of written communication.[1] In this section we will discuss how paragraphs function within a larger work and how they are constructed.

Most compositions have one general theme conveyed by a title. Within its overall framework, however, many separate ideas exist to elaborate upon that theme. The function of a paragraph is to expound upon or explore *one* of these ideas.

The author communicates his intentions in this regard by beginning each paragraph on a new line and indenting the first word of the first sentence about an inch from the left hand margin. The main idea contained in the paragraph is conveyed through a topic sentence which is often the first sentence, but may occupy any position whatever. The remaining sentences exist to provide supporting information and details to round out this central idea.

---

1. Some of the ideas in this section have been adapted from the teaching of Dr. Paul R. Daniels.

At first glance this may appear to be a rather sophisticated concept for a child to be expected to grasp, but surprisingly enough, children tend to group sentences around themes even before they know what paragraphs are. The following activities are designed to build upon this natural ability through a series of steps which will both enable the young writer to recognize, and improve upon, the paragraphs which he composes.

ACTIVITY #1
Recognizing Sentences Which Belong Together

A good introductory activity for the study of paragraphs is to learn to recognize which sentences treat a common idea. The parent begins by writing a topic sentence followed by four or five related sentences and one or two which obviously concern a different subject. Have the child circle the numbers of the sentences that belong together; then write them as a paragraph by indenting the first word of the first sentence.

Below is an example of the type of exercise that you yourself can make up. Provide the child with ample practice in similar exercises until facility is gained in this skill. Then and only then should you proceed to the next activity.

Topic Sentence: Mr. Smith is the nicest man in the neighborhood.

1. Every Monday he helps old Mrs. Johnson do her washing.
2. Wednesdays he drives my mother shopping.
3. Mary bought a pretty new dress.
4. On Saturdays he takes my friends and me to the park.
5. The family next door has a white kitten.

The child should circle sentences numbers 1, 2, and 4 which talk about how nice Mr. Smith is. The copied paragraph should look something like this:

Mr. Smith is the nicest man in the neighborhood. Every Monday he helps old Mrs. Johnson do her washing. Wednesdays he drives my mother shopping. On Saturdays he takes my friends and me to the park.

ACTIVITY #2
Picking Out Sentences Which Don't Stick to the Main Idea

A related activity involves printing or typing a few paragraphs from a story of either your construction or copied from one of the child's books. Insert a sentence in each which really doesn't belong.

BABY ROBINS

The robins' nest was in the tree. Three blue eggs were in the nest. A baby robin came out of each egg. We picked some pretty flowers in our back yard. Now there are three baby robins.

The father and mother robins feed the baby robins. They open their mouths wide to get the food. They like the bugs the big robins give them. They like all the food the mother and father bring. There are other birds in the tree too.

Begin by explaining that in the story above the topic sentence is the first sentence in each paragraph. It indicates the main idea for the paragraph and can be used to help find the sentence which does not belong.

Read the first paragraph aloud once; then go back, point out the topic sentence, and ask if each sentence talks about the nest. The child should have no trouble identifying the one dealing with flowers as not discussing the main idea.

The second paragraph about feeding may be a little more difficult. By using the same sentence-by-sentence questioning technique, however, the child should be able to single out the final one as the outsider.

Before going on, make up other paragraphs for the child to work through in the same way, possibly using examples from earlier writings. Before he can truly understand what a paragraph is, he must be able to recognize what it isn't, so don't progress to the next activity until you feel confident that this skill is mastered.

ACTIVITY #3
Completing Paragraphs

In this activity, topic sentences will be provided with the child being required to write two or three supportive sentences for each one. Be sure each sentence sticks to the main idea of the paragraph. Make up other paragraph ideas to be completed in the same fashion as needed.

ONE DAY IN MY LIFE
In the morning everyone is very busy at my house.

_____

_____

_____

When I get to school there are so many things to do._

_____

_____

_____

After school I go outside to play. _____

_____

_____

ACTIVITY #4
Choosing Topic Sentences

Read the following story out loud to your child. The first paragraph is complete, but the topic sentences are missing in the remaining paragraphs. First, have the child read each paragraph to find out the main idea. Then choose the best candidate for a topic sentence from the three choices, and write it in the blanks. (Answers: 2nd paragraph: 2; 3rd paragraph: 1; 4th paragraph: 3; 5th paragraph: 2).

BABY RABBIT
There was a big forest and in this forest many animals lived. One of these animals was a small baby rabbit. This baby rabbit was named John.

_____

_____

The oak tree was so big that its limbs reached way out like long arms.

1. We like to go to the candy store
2. John lived in a home near a big oak tree in a sunny hillside.
3. John had many friends.

_____

_____

Before John was born Mother Rabbit had carried soft dry leaves to make a thick carpet for the floor. Then she made a pile of leaves in the corner for a bed. On this bed she put soft fur from her own body for a soft warm place to put the tiny baby.

1. Under the oak tree was a hole where John and his mother lived.
2. There are other animals in the forest.
3. We saw ducks at the zoo.

_____

_____

Mother covered him with the warm fur on the bed and fed him with the good milk from her body.

1. The boys kept walking until they saw the oak tree.
2. Birds use twigs to build a nest.
3. When John was born he had no fur and his eyes were closed.

_____

_____

Now he could see how to hop around in his house.

1. Rabbits are cute and have fur.
2. In a few days his eyes opened and his fur began to grow.
3. I like rabbits.

Make up similar exercises on your own or copy paragraphs from books on your child's reading level. Help him read unknown words and discuss each paragraph with which he had trouble.

ACTIVITY #5
Separating Paragraphs

Although your child probably already more or less writes in paragraphs, chances are that he does not recognize that fact and, thus, does not indent them. The purpose of this activity is to teach him to separate paragraphs. Begin by copying consecutive paragraphs from one of his books and requiring him to figure out where one paragraph ends and the other begins.

For example, copy the following passage:

Bob has several pets. He has a cat, a dog, and a pony. His cat Lucy is very shy. Sparkey, his dog, loves to play and jump. Blackie, the pony, always loves to take Bob for a ride. Bob also likes to go see animals at the zoo. His favorite animals are elephants. He laughs when they eat peanuts from his hand.

The child should be able to separate this group of sentences by beginning a new paragraph with "Bob also likes to go . . ." If trouble is encountered, discuss the topic sentences involved in each paragraph and consider all the sentences as they relate to them. (Following several such exercises, you may wish to progress to past examples of the child's own writing which were similarly not separated.)

Once mastered, these five activities should be applied to all your child's writing by either (1) making up additional exercises when you perceive a need or (2) leading him to see how paragraphs in his composition can be improved. As always, however, care must be taken not to emphasize skills such as paragraph construction at the expense of the message the child is trying to communicate.

Dictionary Skills

The further your child advances in writing, the more useful the dictionary will become. It is a veritable reservoir of information, having direct applicability to spelling, vocabulary development, grammatical usage, syllabication, and pronunciation as well as being a formidable source of knowledge in its own right.

Selecting a Dictionary. The chief criteria for selecting a dictionary for your child is the reading level upon which it is written. It will do very little good to teach him to find a word if he cannot understand its definition once found. A second criteria is to make sure that the volume you are considering contains the information your child currently needs without being too difficult. Wide variations exist in this regard and you should examine several dictionaries before selecting one. Points that seem minor, such as size of print and number of words to a page, can make a dictionary appear inviting or overwhelming to a child. The number and quality of pictures may be a factor as well. Bright colors sometimes make a book more appealing, but good black and white drawings can lend an imaginative and attractive quality as well. A dictionary should be a book through which a child *enjoys* leafing.

Other factors to consider are the number of definitions, the presence of pronunciation and syllabication markings, indications of parts of speech, and the spellings of irregular inflected forms (such as plurals). All these things may not be necessary at your child's present stage so use your judgment as to needed features. In recognition of the fact that children may outgrow a dictionary, some companies have series that become progressively more difficult. The illustrations below show how the word *buy* is defined in several commonly used dictionaries. (We have not shown the lowest level picture dictionaries in which a picture may serve instead of words to define an item.) You should make such a comparison on your own before making a purchase.

buy	to get something by giving money for it	*Primary Dictionary Series* Brown, A., Downing, J., and Sceats, J. *Dictionary* 2. New York: Jove/HBJ, 1971. (Ages 6 to 8)
buy	to give money in exchange for something	Same Series, *Dictionary* 3. (Ages 8-10)
buy	to purchase; to get something in exchange for money *buyer* a purchaser	Same Series, *Dictionary* 4. (Ages 10-12)
buy	get by paying some money: You can buy a pencil for school. *bought, buy ing.*	*My Second Picture Dictionary* Greet, W.C., Jenkins, W.A., & Schiller, A. New York: Lothrop, Lee & Shepard Company, 1971.
buy	(bī), 1 get by paying a price; purchase: *You can buy a pencil for five cents.* 2 bargain: *That book was a real buy.* 1 verb, *bought, buying;* 2 noun.	*Scott, Foresman Beginning Dictionary.* Thorndike, E.L., & Barnhart, C.L. New York: Doubleday & Company, 1976.
buy	to get something by paying money for it: purchase. John can *buy* an ice-cream cone for twenty-five cents. Our family *bought* a new car last year. *Verb.*—A bargain. That used car is a good *buy. Noun* Another word that sounds like this is *by.* buy (bī) verb, *bought buying;* noun plural *buys.*	*Macmillan Dictionary for Children.* Halsey, W.D. (Editorial Director), Morris, C.G. (Ed.) New York: Macmillan Publishing Co., Inc. 1976.
¹buy ²buy	/'bī/vb *bought* /'bȯt/; *buy • ing:* to get by paying for: PURCHASE—*buy•er* n n: something bought at a favorable price	*Webster's New Elementary Dictionary.* Springfield, Mass.: G & C Merriam Co., Publishers, 1975.

Alphabetical Order. Learning alphabetical order includes a heirarchy of skills which should be taught gradually as the need for using the dictionary increases. The activities which follow encompass the basic skills needed for locating alphabetically listed words. Chances are that your child will have already attained some of these skills, thus you should only teach the ones not yet mastered.

ACTIVITY #1
Teaching the Concept of Alphabetical Order

Since your child can already recite the alphabet, this activity should be very easy for him. Its purpose is to simply underline the fact that the order in which the alphabet was learned has significance in its own right.

Place a copy of the alphabet in front of the child, using one of the alphabet strips discussed in Chapter Two if convenient. Discuss the alphabet with the child, such as the fact that it begins with **A,** ends with **Z,** and has twenty-six letters in all. Point to each as they are counted, then ask the following questions using the alphabet as a reference, guiding the child in searching from *left* to *right* for particular letters.

1. Which letter comes first, A or Z?
2. Which letter comes second?
3. What is the next letter after C?
4. What letter comes right before H?
5. Which letter comes first, F or M?

Continue asking questions such as this until your child can answer without hesitation.

ACTIVITY #2
Putting Letters in Order

Write different combinations of letters in mixed-up order with blanks beside them. Have the child rewrite the letters in alphabetical order in the provided blanks. In the beginning you may allow him to refer to his alphabet list but you will, of course, gradually want to wean him away from this dependence. Provide as much practice as needed.

B	F	C
A ___ ___ ___	A ___ ___ ___	Z ___ ___ ___
C	R	U

Once the child becomes proficient in this activity you may wish to teach him in which part of the alphabet different letters are located. To do this, divide an alphabet strip into two halves:

ABCDEFGHIJKLM   NOPQRSTUVWXYZ

Dictate letters to the child asking him in which half of the alphabet they belong, first or second. Compliment him when he is right, allow him to look the letter up when he is incorrect.

ACTIVITY #3
Alphabetizing by the First Letter

Write the following words on index cards and have the child place the three cards of each group in alphabetical order. As in the previous activity, allow him to refer to his alphabet list, but encourage less and less dependence upon it.

(2) be	(3) some	(1) away
(3) come	(2) get	(3) took
(1) at	(1) can	(2) have

The following words make sentences when they are arranged horizontally in order.

(2) boy	(3) zoo
(1) a	(2) the
(3) can	(1) see
(4) run	

Variations of this activity include taking out selected words from the Word Box and asking the child to refile them in alphabetical order. In addition certain words can be named for location in the Word Box, in a Picture Dictionary, or glossary.

ACTIVITY #4
Alphabetizing by the First Two Letters

Explain to the child that when the first letter in words is the same, they are put in alphabetical order by the second letter.

EXAMPLE: (2) at   Look at the second letter in each word.
            (1) are   Since *r* comes before *t, are* comes before *at*.

Other words to put in order:

(2) at	(4) funny	(1) again	(2) give
(3) away	(1) father	(3) and	(3) go
(1) are	(3) friends	(2) all	(1) get
	(2) fish		(4) green
(2) they	(1) ball	(4) would	(1) many
(4) tree	(2) be	(3) when	(4) must
(3) too	(4) boy	(2) we	(3) morning
(1) tall	(3) big	(1) walk	(2) me

Make up similar exercises for words beginning with the same two or three letters when this skill has been mastered. Also explain how words such as *help* and *helpful* are alphabetized (*help* comes first).

Putting the child's alphabetizing skills to work. Once the child understands the concept of alphabetizing and can complete the exercises above, he should be ready to find words in the dictionary. The first step is to obtain a beginning dictionary which can be read comfortably as discussed above. (Your librarian or an elementary school teacher would also be a good source of advice for locating an appropriate volume.)

Once it is obtained, sit down with your child, discuss what a dictionary is used for, and show him how to use the guide words. (They indicate the first and last words on each page.) The child must decide if the word he seeks falls between those two words. Look a few up together and read the definitions with him. If a picture dictionary has been constructed earlier, or the Word Box sorted to check the spelling of words needed for writing, chances are that no difficulty will be encountered here.

If trouble is encountered, the task can be simplified by practicing locating a word on one page or in one column. Another way to make dictionary use easier is to remind the child in which part of the alphabet (first half/second half) a beginning letter resides (and hence in which approximate section of the dictionary a word is likely to be).

As with most types of learning, the only real way for the child to become comfortable using the dictionary is through continual practice over a long period of time. Ensure that once he learns how, he uses the dictionary on a regular basis to both look up the meaning of new words encountered in reading and the spelling of words needed for writing. Later, as more and more proficiency is attained, you may demonstrate other features of the dictionary, such as the meaning of diacritical markings, accents, syllabication, choosing the best definition for a particular setting, and so forth. (A good dictionary will explain its various uses on the first several pages.)

9

Cursive Writing

Learning to write in cursive style is an exciting time for children. It signals putting one foot into the adult world, for it cannot escape the child's attention that grown-ups write much faster and differently than they, using fancy, connected strokes.

It was not always so. The teaching of manuscript writing (printing) was initiated by an English educator at the beginning of this century and exported to Boston and New York in 1921. Before that all school children were taught cursive writing in the first grade.

The original justification for teaching children to print was based on the arguments that it (1) is more legible than cursive, (2) is easier for children to learn, (3) is more rhythmical to write, (4) facilitates learning to read and spell, and (5) constitutes an excellent basis for the transition to cursive if desired. Parents of that time were far from convinced, however, citing the need for cursive writing in the business world and the fear that if children only wrote in manuscript they could not read cursive.

The proponents of manuscript writing eventually won out. Children are taught to print as early as kindergarten and normally taught cursive only at the end of second or beginning of third grade. From a practical point of view, cursive writing no longer serves as crucial a function in everyday life (and especially the

204

business world) as it did before the widespread use of the typewriter. Nevertheless a decent cursive style is important to the child throughout his schooling career where the shape of handwriting often influences how well the contents of written assignments are received (and even how test answers are graded). After school, the nonfluent typist uses cursive for all correspondences and, even when a secretary is available, an illegible handwriting style may be a real liability. (Surveys of secretaries have reported that illegible writing accounts for an amazing amount of lost time, money, and embarrassing mistakes.)

Regardless of how crucial it becomes later, however, the immediate reality is that your child is going to have to learn to write in cursive in the early grades. That task can be made easier by helping him learn at home.

Introduction to Cursive Writing

The child who has no difficulty writing legible manuscript forms from memory is usually ready to begin learning cursive. Before learning to write in cursive, familiarity with the letter forms is helpful. You will need to make a concentrated effort to write very clearly and simply, checking your letters against those in the illustration on page 206.

A good way to begin is through informal exposure to the child's first name written in cursive. Use opportunities such as birthday, Christmas, and other greeting cards to show him his name. Write it as a label or sign it as proof of ownership on books and toys.

Once the child has seen his name in cursive several times, point to each letter in order from left to right, saying them out loud. Print the name; then write it directly below for easy comparison.

Johnny

Johnny

ALPHABET CHART

Talk about how cursive slants and uses curving strokes which connect one letter to the next while manuscript letters do neither. If the child wants to write his name in cursive, by all means show him how. Before you do so, however, study the section below entitled, "The Correct Position for Cursive Writing."

Recognizing the Cursive Alphabet

Prepare word cards in manuscript letters for the following words by printing one word on the top half of each card and leaving the bottom half blank:

dad	the	run	zoo	big
a	book	quit	box	I
dog	fell	name	very	good
it	see	jump	is	me
cow	us	you	my	exit

Present the cards to the child one by one. Put those he can read in one pile and those he cannot in another. Look at each word in the "don't know" pile. If it is a noun or verb, write the word again on the back of the card leaving space for a picture at the top (with words like "a" and "very" pictures are not appropriate, of course). Have the child participate in coming up with a picture clue and draw it above the word. (Don't worry about quality as long as the pictures are recognizable). Some sample ideas for these pictures might be:

dad:	man's face
dog:	a dog
see:	a pair of eyes with glasses
us:	a parent with a child
run:	a person running
quit:	a child walking away from other children playing
name:	your child's name

For those words which the child cannot read, spend as much time as necessary practicing reading the picture side of the card, then the side with only the word. When most of the words are recognized, write each in cursive on the front of the cards directly below the printed version.

As the child looks on, take each card and point to the cursive letters in order (from left to right) while spelling the word aloud. Have the child join in when he can. If he has difficulty, direct him to look at the printed letters first as clues. Work on each card until all the letters can be pointed out and named (reference to the printed clues can be continued if necessary).

Next, present the cards one-by-one as you *cover up* the printed version of each with your hand. If the child cannot read the word, uncover the print. If even that version has been forgotten, turn the card over for a picture clue. You should continue in this fashion, perhaps for several lessons, until most of the words are identified in cursive styles. (We say *most* because there will be ample practice later for those letters not easily learned.)

How to Use This Chapter

In some ways teaching cursive writing is like teaching two subjects instead of one. As with printing, upper and lower case forms of the same letter often diverge widely. Unlike printing, the cursive upper case forms are usually considerably more difficult than their lower case counterparts. Also unlike printing, the lower case letters and most of the capitals connect to one another. (The fact that some capitals do not connect is always confusing to beginners.)

Because of these differences, therefore, the cursive lessons will be organized differently than those in Chapter Two. All the lower case letters will be taught before any capitals are introduced. This means that if your child wishes to write cursive sentences before all the capitals are learned, he will have to *substitute a printed for a cursive capital.*

Since your child is no longer a handwriting novice, we will introduce several letters sharing similar characteristics in each lesson. As always, however, there is a great deal of flexibility as to how much content needs to be covered how quickly. Each lesson therefore contains many natural breaking points. You may wish, for example, to cover one *letter* a day or less, spreading the lessons out, and interspersing them with the ongoing writing activities discussed in previous chapters. Fifteen minutes spent on cursive writing per day is usually plenty. Whatever pace you opt for, remember to allow ample time to review both new and old material.

Lesson Format

Although each lesson contains more than one letter to be learned, each letter is taught alone before it is combined with other forms. The basic sequence of teaching steps are as follows:

1. The letter is introduced by its placement within the alphabet strip (see Materials below) and via an appropriate word card (see Recognizing the Cursive Alphabet above),
2. an exercise sheet is presented to the child for tracing, completing, and free writing practice along with oral instructions to facilitate the task,
3. "cautions" are available to you, the teacher, which point out common mistakes often made in forming a particular letter, and
4. "adding meaning" exercises are presented which teach the child to write words and sentences in cursive.

Detailed instructions are presented only for teaching the first letter ("c") and the first "adding meaning" activity (which does not appear until "d" is introduced). After that only new information will be presented. You will make up an exercise sheet for each letter in accordance with the example on page 211 by simply substituting the letter being taught. To keep all the teaching procedures fresh in your mind, you may need to review the model lesson from time to time.

Practice

Practice only makes perfect in handwriting if it is properly supervised. Bad habits learned early can remain for a lifetime, so it is more important that your child make the transition from printing to cursive writing correctly than it is that he do so early. Make sure that all letters can be correctly formed *before* you encourage your child to use cursive in his everyday writing and, even then, be on the lookout for stylistic abnormalities in need of remediation. Factors to look for when analyzing handwriting quality include: letter size, uniformity of slant, evenness of spacing and position on the line. The earlier problems are identified the easier they are to correct.

The Correct Position for Cursive Writing

The only difference in positions for printing and cursive writing is in that of the paper. When printing, the page lies straight up and down (or perpendicular) to the body. In cursive writing, the paper is slanted to produce a slant in the writing. Righthanded writers slant the paper to the left so that the bottom left hand corner points to the center of the body. Lefthanded writers slant the paper to the right so that the bottom righthand corner points to the left elbow. As he did with printing, the lefthanded writer keeps the paper slightly to the left of the desk's center. If learning to slant letters to the right becomes an impossible task, a vertical style or even left slant should be permitted.

All children start out using two spaces on the page for tall letters and one space for small letters. For the proper way to sit, hold the pencil, and adjust lighting, see Chapter Two.

Materials

The materials you will need to teach the lessons in this chapter follow. As always, make sure that everything (including prepared exercise sheets) is available before you actually sit down to teach.

1. *Pencils* with erasers.
2. *Lined Paper* with lines ½ inch apart.
3. *3" × 5" Index Cards* (or larger) with sample words as described in "Recognizing Cursive Writing" above.
4. *An Alphabet Strip* containing each of the upper case letters followed by their lower case counterparts written in cursive. It can consist of strips of paper taped together or of wide masking tape affixed to the child's desk or table.
5. *Exercise Sheets* prepared on lined paper for the child to complete. You should construct these sheets for each letter

modeled exactly upon the one depicted below. If more practice is needed than these exercises afford, simply make up additional sheets.

CURSIVE EXERCISE SHEET

6. *Adding Meaning Exercise Sheets* also prepared on lined paper for the child to complete. You should prepare each exercise based upon the example below. The first line should always contain the complete word written several times for the child to trace. The next three lines will progressively require less tracing and more completing on the child's part with the last part of the last line requiring him to write the entire word.

ADDING MEANING EXERCISE SHEET

LESSON #1
Writing the Letters c, a, d, o, g, and q

These six lower case letters will be taught in sequence because they all have similar starting points. All begin with the pencil on the middle line moving in a circular motion to the left as illustrated by the letter c.

c   Model Lesson

WORD CARDS: *cow*

Have the child locate the lower case **c** on his cursive alphabet strip. Hold his index finger as you would a pencil and trace it slowly, using the same starting point and sequence of strokes which are used in writing. Next, give him the word cards to sort through for any words containing the letter **c**. There is only one: *cow*.

PRACTICE: See Illustration on page 211.

Present your copy of the exercise on a sheet of tablet paper. With the blunt end of your pencil demonstrate the correct sequence of strokes by tracing the first **c**. Talk about the letter, pointing out where it starts. You may then allow the child to trace the *disconnected* **c**'s on the first line and continue by tracing one and writing two on the second and third lines. Make sure that you say, and encourage the child to say, the name of each letter as it is completed.

GUIDE WORDS: down-up/go back down-up/ . . .

After you are sure the child can construct disconnected **c**'s show him (with the blunt end of your pencil) how to trace the pairs of *connected* **c**'s on line four using the proper sequence of strokes. Talk about the letter, pointing out where it starts (at the line when disconnected) and what is involved in connecting it (in this case the top of the **c** must "be retraced" as indicated by the guide words "go back down"). As this is done you may help by repeating the guide words: "down-up-go back down-up go back . . ." Gradually lower your voice and finally stop saying them altogether when you are sure that the correct sequence of strokes is being followed. (Some children find this helpful; some do not. We have included them only for the first several letters. If you wish to continue the practice, you will have no trouble making up your own.) On the remaining row, the pair of **c**'s will be traced and the blank space filled in by the child with other parts of connected **c**'s.

Observe the child closely as he traces. If necessary, put your hand over his, guiding him in the correct movements. Remind him that the **c** must touch the middle and bottom lines and after each row is completed call attention to which letters are done best and why. If there is any question in your mind as to whether or not a letter has been mastered, provide an additional practice page and repeat the process.

a

WORD CARDS: *a* (Point out that "a" is both a letter and a word.)

GUIDE WORDS: down-up-straight back down/up-down-up-straight back down/ . . .

CAUTION: Be sure that the child does not lift his pencil while forming the letter, and ensure that the circle is closed.

d

WORD CARDS: *dad, dog*

GUIDE WORDS: down-up-go back down/up-down-up-go back down/ . . .

CAUTION: Be sure that the stick of the **d** is retraced accurately so a simple line results (not a loop). As with the **a** make sure that the pencil is not lifted so that the circle is closed.

Adding Meaning

Present the word card for "dad" and have the child spell it aloud. Next, show the child the *Adding Meaning Exercise Sheet* you have made (see page 211) pointing out the spacing between the words. Have the child trace what is there and add what is missing so that all three letters are always made in order. You will, of course, be vigilant that the correct sequence of strokes is followed.

o

COMMENTS: The letter **o** is made very similarly to the **a** except the circle is rounder and the last line is horizontal rather than vertical.

WORD CARDS: *dog, cow, book, you, zoo, box, good*

GUIDE WORDS: down-up-over/down-up-over . . .

CAUTION: The **o** should be round and end in a flat stroke whether connected or disconnected.

g

COMMENTS: The **g** begins like the other letters in this group before swinging down and looping to the left.

WORD CARDS: *dog, good*

CAUTION: The circle must be closed before the swing down is begun.

q

COMMENTS: Made like the **g** until the downward slope which goes straight down before it loops up toward the *right.*

WORD CARDS: *quit*

CAUTION: As with the **g** the circle must be closed before starting down. The tail must be pulled down straight for the loop to the right to look different from the **g**.

LESSON #2
Writing the Letters **i, t, u,** and **w.**

The four letters **i, t, u,** and **w** are taught as a group because they all start at the baseline and require similar retracing movements. Retracing here means that you make a stroke and then go back down over it before proceeding.

i

COMMENTS: The letter **i** will serve as a good preparatory exercise for the other letters since it is essentially the first stroke in them all.

WORD CARDS: *it, is, big, quit*

CAUTION: Retracing must be done carefully so that only one line results. Also, since in normal writing isolated lower case **i**'s do not exist, you should remember that the **i** is normally dotted only after the word in which it appears is completed. In practicing its formation, therefore, have all the connected **i**'s dotted after each sequence.

ADDING

MEANING: The **i** will be incorporated into the "Adding Meaning" exercise for **t** below.

t

COMMENTS: Like the printed version, the **t** does not reach all the way to the top line. Its trunk is made exactly like the **i** except it is taller.

CAUTION: Like the **i** the **t** must be retraced carefully to avoid two lines resulting. It should be crossed above the middle line and, like the dot for the **i**, the letter should normally be crossed only after completion of the word in which it appears.

WORD CARDS: *it, quit, the*

ADDING

MEANING: Present the above cards and ask the child which word he could write in cursive. When he identifies *it*, allow him to complete the standard "Adding Meaning" exercise.

u

COMMENTS: This letter should be relatively easy to learn because it is really no different than two connected **i**'s without the dots.

WORD CARDS: *us, run, quit, jump*

CAUTION: The two lines must be retraced carefully.

ADDING

MEANING: *quit*

w

COMMENTS: The **w** is made like two connected **u**'s without the final line retraced. The final stroke of the **w** is horizontal like that of the **o**. *It is therefore a good idea to review the* **o** *before teaching the* **w**.

WORD CARDS: *cow*

CAUTION: The first stroke of the **w** is retraced except when it follows **b**, **o**, or **v**, or when connecting **w**'s for practice.

ADDING
MEANING: Make an exercise sheet for cow.

REVIEW: First have the child practice writing **c**, **a**, **d**, **o**, and **g** as disconnected letters. Next, write the following silly sentence for the child in cursive:

A cow got a dog.

Little trouble should be encountered with the upper case **a** since it is identical to its lower case counterpart save for the fact that it reaches all the way to the top line. You may wish, however, to give the child some practice with it by making up an exercise sheet (see Illustration p. 224 for the proper letter formation).

Once the capital **a** can be formed comfortably, have the child copy the above sentence until fluency is obtained. It does not have to fit on one line so be sure that he spaces adequately between words.

LESSON #3
Writing the Letters 3, l, h, k, b, and f

The letters **e**, **l**, **h**, **k**, **b**, and **f** have been grouped together because they are all what we call "upper loop letters," meaning they all contain loops above the baseline. In fact, this upper loop, starting at the baseline, is the first stroke involved in each letter.

e

COMMENT: The letter **e** serves as an excellent introduction and preparatory activity for the other five members of this group since it involves the simplest loop stroke, and is the same size as the previously learned letters.

WORD CARDS: *the, fell, see, name, very*

CAUTION: The loop should be watched carefully. It should first bear toward the right, touch the midline, then actually loop over to the left before bearing toward the right again. The letter both begins and ends on the baseline.

ADDING

MEANING: The **e** will be used in the "Adding Meaning" exercise for **f** below.

l

COMMENT: The letter **l** is still the basic loop learned through making the **e**, only taller and narrower.

WORD CARDS: *fell*

CAUTION: The loop should extend up to the top line and cross itself below the midline.

ADDING

MEANING: The **l** will also be used in the "Adding Meaning" exercise for **f**.

h

COMMENT: The letter **h** involves a variation upon the basic loop in which the final part comes straight down (or even bears slightly to the left), leaving room for the hump. This is not a particularly easy letter and may require more practice than usual.

WORD CARDS: *the*

CAUTION: Make sure that the loop is made correctly. If it is made in the same way as the other letters, there will be no room for the hump, which should start at the baseline and touch the midline at its peak.

ADDING

MEANING: Make an exercise sheet for *the*.

k

COMMENT: The letter **k** is formed identically to **h** with one slight variation. It is best taught by having the child begin with the letter **h**. You can then trace over his effort with a red pen to illustrate how they differ.

WORD CARDS: *book*

CAUTION: Make sure that the child closes the hump by touching the loop somewhere just below the mid-line.

ADDING
MEANING: The **k** will be practiced in the "Adding Meaning" exercise for **b**.

b

COMMENTS: The letter **b** begins with the basic **l** loop, varying only after the entire stroke is completed. Have the child draw an **l**. As with the last letter, you can then trace over it with a red pen illustrating the variation.

WORD CARDS: *book, box, big*

CAUTION: Note that the final horizontal stroke of the **b** is like that of the **o** and **w**. Do not allow the child to bring it back down toward the baseline.

ADDING
MEANING: Review the **o** and **k** before making an exercise to sheet for *book*.

f

COMMENTS: The letter **f** combines elements from the basic upper loop common to all the letters in this lesson and the lower loop from the **g**. Before teaching, review the **g** and then the **h**.

WORD CARDS: *fell*

CAUTION: Make sure that two distinct loops are formed: one like that of the **h** crossing itself at or below the midline, the other like the **g**. Each loop should, in other words, balloon in the same direction.

ADDING
MEANING: Make an exercise sheet for *fell*.

REVIEW: Have the child practice writing the following

sentence until fluency is attained since it reviews all the letters taught in Lesson #3.

The book fell.

Make sure the proper spacing between words is maintained as well as the relative sizes of letters. As we mentioned earlier, you may wish to simply allow the child to substitute a printed **T** in this exercise until the capital cursive version is taught. (If you prefer, however, you may turn to Part Two and teach the capital **T** here.)

LESSON #4
Writing the letters s and r.

The letters **s** and **r** are taught together because they both start and end at the baseline as well as touch the midline with a peak or point.

s

WORD CARDS:	*see, us, is*
CAUTION:	Make sure that the top of the letter ends in a point touching the midline. The s itself is closed with the bottom section being retraced.
ADDING MEANING:	Make an exercise sheet for *see*.

r

WORD CARDS:	*run, very*
CAUTION:	The **r** has two points with only the first touching the midline, the second slightly below it and to the right.
ADDING MEANING:	The **r** will be applied in the "Adding Meaning" exercise for **n**.

LESSON #5
Writing the letters n, m, x, and v

These four letters should be taught together because they all involve variations of a new stroke which we will call the "bump."

n

COMMENTS:	The letter **n** employs two bumps back to back.
WORD CARDS:	*run, name*
CAUTION:	The side of the first bump must be *retraced* to make the second one.
ADDING MEANING:	Make an exercise sheet for *run*.

m

COMMENTS:	The letter **m** is identical to the **n** except it employs three bumps. If your child has trouble remembering the distinction, you might have him count them as he forms the letter.
WORD CARDS:	*name, my, me*
CAUTION:	This letter may be confused with the **n**. Also remember that two strokes are retraced.
ADDING MEANING:	Make an exercise sheet for *name*.

x

COMMENTS:	While the letter **x** appears to be the simplest of the bump letters, it is complicated by the cross mark which children are often inclined to either forget or make in the wrong direction.
WORD CARDS:	*box*
CAUTION:	Make sure the entire word is written before the **x** is crossed. Sometimes verbalizing "cross the **x**" helps the child remember to do it in the early stages of cursive writing.
ADDING MEANING:	Make an exercise sheet for *box*. (Note that the **x** loses one of its sides when connected to an **o**.

v

COMMENT:	The letter **v** is quite similar to the **x**. Show the child that to make a **v** he can start to make an **x** and just make the final tail "come up high."
WORD CARDS:	*very*
CAUTION:	The **v** connects in the same way that the **o** does, with a horizontal tail. You may wish to review the **o** for this characteristic.
ADDING MEANING:	Point out that the **e** changes shape when connected to the **v** (it would do the same thing connected to an **o**, of course), then make an exercise sheet for *very*.
REVIEW:	Have the following sentence written to attain fluency.

The box is very big.

PART II

Teaching the Capital Letters

Most of the capital cursive letters are quite similar to their manuscript counterparts, simply being less angular and more flowing. Some are quite aberrant, however, such as the **F, I, L, Q, T,** and **Z**. (The **A** and **J**, while different from print, are similar to their lower case cursive counterparts). To further make life a little more difficult for you, some capitals connect to lower case letters in words and some do not (**D, O, P, T, U, V,** and **W**).

Since capital letters are not used in writing as often as lower case ones, they may take longer to master. Your chief task at this point is to insure that your child knows the proper sequence of strokes going into the formation of each letter, practices them sufficiently, and then incorporates the letter into his regular writing activities. (When the child writes on his own, have a cursive alphabet strip in view so that he can refresh his memory for little used forms.)

Since you have logged considerable teaching practice by now, we are only going to include the bare minimum of information

Cursive Capitals:
Instructional Order and Adding Meaning Activities

Teaching Order	Suggested Adding Meaning Activities
C	Christmas
E	Easter
O	October
A	August
M	Mary
N	November
H	Halloween
K	Kate
L	Linda
P	Paul
B	Bill
R	Ray
T	Tom
F	Friday
D	December
G	George
S	September
U	USA
V	Valentine's Day
W	Wednesday
X	Xmas
Q	Queen Ann
I	Indian
J	January
Y	New Year's Day
Z	Zorro

needed to teach the capital letters in the form of a chart especially constructed for the purpose, containing the order in which the letters should be taught and suggested adding meaning activities. (The correct sequences of strokes are contained in the illustration on page 224. The basic lesson format will remain identical to that employed with the lower case letters:

1. the letter in question is located in the alphabet strip and traced with your guidance,
2. an exercise sheet based upon the illustration on page 211 is completed (remember to prepare additional exercises if needed),
3. actual writing practice ("adding meaning") involving the letter is engaged in, and
4. review activities are conducted at the end of each lesson.

PART III

Supplementary Activities

The lessons in the first two parts of this chapter will give your child the essential practice he needs to form the cursive alphabet. Every child, however, will have special, individual problems distinguishing between certain letters, connecting especially difficult combinations of letters, and so forth. You will, therefore, quite naturally provide additional instruction and practice in these trouble spots.

Below are a few suggested areas where we have found most children in need of additional practice. Undoubtedly, you will be able to add to this list.

1. connect the lower case **o** to every letter in the alphabet:
2. Connect **S, G, B,** to **a,** then **i:**
3. Connect **w** to all the vowels:
4. Make a row of **T**'s followed by a row of **F**'s:
5. Make a row of **I**'s, then a row of **J**'s:

10

Conclusion

By choosing to follow the program in this book you have decided to seize the initiative in your child's education. It is a wise decision, but not an easy one. The path you have chosen is both time-consuming and fraught with difficulty; it also happens to be about the only one that a parent who really cares about his child's achievement can conscientiously take in these times.

In our concluding chapter of *Teach Your Child To Read*, the first book in this series, we discussed the importance of maintaining the momentum which the parent had generated by taking his child's education into his own hands. As important as this is in reading, it is even more crucial for your child's future writing success.

Once a child can read comfortably at a certain level, the activity is, at least to a certain extent, self-reinforcing and self-perpetuating in its own right. Children enjoy reading on their own and usually improve on their own with enough help and encouragement. Writing, as a subject, is not quite so accomodating.

In the first place, it is not nearly as likely to be self-reinforcing. A child finds sitting down and reading a *Nancy Drew* mystery far more rewarding than trying to write one. Writing requires a sympathetic audience; reading is providing it to someone else.

Because your child's skills are extremely limited now, and will be for years to come, *you* must provide that audience. It is a rare child indeed who will write solely for himself; it is even rarer for continued improvement to occur without constant feedback and instruction in the mechanics of the process. The reason is simple: writing is harder than reading. Not to teach, but to do.

We have discussed only the most rudimentary writing skills in this book, skills which many children can be expected to master by the end of their eighth year or sooner. There is much, much more the child will need to learn before he becomes an accomplished writer. We have not dealt with many aspects of grammar, such as parts of speech, clauses, participles, moods, the more complex verb tenses, and so forth. These must come later, but they are so heavily influenced by the oral language the child hears in his home that even now you are having a greater role in their teaching than you suspect. When the time does come for your child to learn more complex skills, you will be able to help him by applying the techniques learned here to the relevant sections of his language arts textbooks.

Thus, although there is a great deal more your child will need to know as he progresses, there will be plenty of time as long as you continue the momentum already achieved. To do otherwise is to squander your investment.

To truly protect this investment you also must not neglect your child's other basic skills, especially reading. Continued writing improvement is heavily dependent upon your child's reading development. If you feel that he does not read as well or as much as he should, you might consider trying the reading program in our first book. The child who does not read will not long continue to write.

We hope that you have enjoyed, and will continue to enjoy, helping your child learn to write. The foundations for long term growth are all contained in this book: stimuli for writing in Chapter Four, to which you and your child will undoubtedly be able to add; sentence construction in Chapter Five, which may be the single most important skill for the two of you to continue working on; spelling and vocabulary development in Chapters Six and Seven, skills and attributes which grow naturally with age and reading growth and thus can be enhanced with a minimum of effort on your part; and finally, paragraph formation in Chapter Eight, which is an